CHRIST
AND THE
PRISONER'S
WIFE

KATHLEEN DONALSON TAYLER

ISBN 979-8-89112-928-3 (Paperback)
ISBN 979-8-89112-929-0 (Digital)

Covenant Books
11661 Hwy 707
Murrells Inlet, SC 29576
www.covenantbooks.com

CONTENTS

ACKNOWLEDGMENTS

Dean, you are the love of my life. I'm so proud of the man you are today. I know this story is difficult for you, but you would rather sacrifice your own feelings to bring people to Christ than hide the past.

Dad and Mom: Mom, I finally wrote it! You have been telling me for years to write a book. I think the content is going to be more than you expected or knew. Thank you for standing by me. Even more, thank you for continually praying for me. Dad, thank you for embracing Dean as your son.

Grandma Hagood will never see this recognition or book. She is with Jesus. I would be remiss if I did not acknowledge her godly influence in my life. She was a prayer warrior and taught me how to pray and journal. My prayer journals were the conception of this book.

My boys—Coy, J.R., and C.J.—you are such a blessing in my life. I watch all three of you, and I'm in awe of what fantastic dads you are to your kids.

Nickie, my best friend and sister in Christ, you have been in my life more than thirty-five years. You encourage me daily and draw me closer to Christ. I'm so proud of you and your influence for the kingdom of God. You truly are a Proverbs 31 woman.

The pastors of Calvary—Pastor Ray, Pastor Jason, and Pastor Shaun—you three men have been extremely influential in our lives. You took a chance on us and discipled us. You taught me the role of the man as a spiritual leader and imparted more wisdom to me more than you will even realize.

PROLOGUE

I belonged to a secret club, a club no one wishes to join. Membership requires one to be a family member of a prisoner. We are out there: at work, at church, at the park, in the grocery store, and rarely do those around us know that our life includes visits to a prison. Our colleagues try to set us up on dates. Club members never ask, "What are they in prison for?" or "What did they do?" Instead, we offer words of comfort to one another in the halls, walking toward the visiting room, and ask, "How much longer?"

Big Daddy Weave sings a song called "My Story" (2015).

> If I told you my story
> You would hear Hope that wouldn't let go
> Oh to tell you my story is to tell of Him

God writes his story in our lives if we surrender to him. His story in my life is one of forgiveness, redemption, and reconciliation, thus was birthed the story of *Christ and the Prisoner's Wife*. The story is true. Although many names have been changed to protect individuals, the intent is not to cause any harm. I had kept prayer journals, letters, and other documents. The items included in the story are all authentic, although several documents are abbreviated with only portions included.

⸺◈⸺

CHAPTER 1

A Dark December Night

I woke startled. I looked at the clock and saw it was almost 2:00 a.m. The loud noise had shaken me to the core; my heart was racing. I hurried downstairs to check the boys, thinking that my oldest, Coy, must be up and fired the gunshot. We lived out in the country, and coyote visits were frequent. Coy was only fourteen years old, but he was an excellent shot. He often used the gun to kill rattlesnakes. Coy and J.R. were asleep in their beds. Our border collie mix, Rodeo, was fast asleep in the entryway. The noise had woken me so suddenly and was so loud. How could the dog and kids all be asleep?

I returned to my bedroom. I wondered if I had imagined the noise or perhaps had a bad dream. I sat on my bed, unable to calm my racing heart. I was still shaking. I heard that still, small voice and saw a vision of God's hands reaching down, "I've got you." The voice was not audible. Nonetheless, I knew God was talking to me. The vision, not in front of my eyes but, in my mind, a clear picture and one I could not have imagined in that moment. I finally settled back in my bed. I lay awake, praying for hours, "Lord, what does that mean? What are you trying to tell me?" Finally, I drifted back to sleep.

When morning came, the phone rang. The lady was a friend that "heard the story" and was calling to talk about the night's events. Dean had been 230 miles away and was picked up by the police. Her husband had been at the scene. Later I would discover he too was involved. The situation was beyond description, and at that moment, my life changed. The time of the incident was just before 2:00 a.m., December 2006. How could I have possibly heard the gunshot? The rest of the conversation was a blur. She continued to talk, but I could not comprehend her words. J.R. (who was eleven years old) was sitting in a chair in the living room, watching my expressions and listening to the end of the conversation. He started crying and asking me, "Mom, what happened?" I could not respond. I dropped the phone and went out to the driveway and locked myself in the car. I called Dean's father. He had not heard anything but told me he would call the police and get back to me. I have no idea how long I stayed in the car, crying and in disbelief. I later found out that J.R. had ran out to the backfield across the cactus barefoot, with only a T-shirt and his undershorts on, and sat in the field for hours. I find it hard to understand now how I did not even know where my kids were, how they were processing the information, and how I was absent from helping them to cope. The boys found out information from other kids, people that lived in the same town as Dean and knew the boys. At the time, I experienced that sensation, where time stood still, and the world around me was in slow motion. I compared it to the sensation that occurred when I was once in a car accident in college. The car crashed against the railing of the interstate and then spiraled back across traffic. Everything was a blur. My life had just crashed, and it seemed incomprehensible. Dean's father finally called back. He had no details of the situation, only that Dean had indeed been arrested and was in the county jail.

My walk with Christ would be challenged, strengthened, and tested to my very core. One day at a time, and thus, at that moment, I would become the prisoner's wife. In Psalm 56:8, David stated, "You keep track of all my sorrows. You have collected all my tears in your bottle. You have recorded each one in your book." God collected a lot of my tears over the years. That December evening, it snowed. I looked up and felt like God was weeping with me.

The following day, I tried to fill the next day with activity to occupy the boys and me. We put up Christmas lights around the outside of the house, although we were far from being jolly or in the

Christmas spirit. I choked back the tears and refused to talk about the situation. I know now the best thing would have been to talk to my kids, sit with them, pray with them. With heartbreak, I reflect that in those moments, I failed. I had not heard from Dean. He was allowed a phone call, and that phone call was not to me. At dusk, the boys and I came in from outside. That December day had been cold and chilly. I started making hot cocoa for all of us and turned on the news. There on the television was Dean's mug shot as the news reporter told the story briefly. The man in the photo looked so different than the man I once knew. I felt as if I was in a nightmare, and at any moment, I would wake up.

I pondered how the kids would possibly return to school on Monday and deal with this situation or how I would return to work. How would we answer the questions? I was positive Dean would make bail and be back in a few days. The thought terrified me. I did not want Dean back in my life or in the boys' lives. Maybe I would finally be free. I called my sister and parents. My mother jumped in a car and drove to our home 250 miles away. She stayed several days. My sister, Kay, told me to just pack up the kids and leave the state for a while. She would pay for plane tickets to come to Arizona. Christmas was coming, and the boys and I could celebrate Christmas there. I took her up on the offer, and we left the state. I just could not bear to see the newspaper articles online or hear the story on the broadcast news again, and I certainly did not want my boys to see or hear anymore.

I pleaded with God to change the vision. He needed to hold my boys in his hands and not me. He had to take care of my boys. Many sleepless nights followed. I could not eat or sleep. First Thessalonians 5:17 states to "pray without ceasing." I certainly had that concept down. I prayed continually. Even now as I reflect, those days and weeks seem like such a blur. I have these huge gaps in my memory. Hours turned to days, and days turned to weeks, and weeks turned into months. The boys and I were functioning in a daze. Our world had been drastically changed in a moment.

CHAPTER 2

A Marriage of Turmoil

Dean was 6'3", with sandy blonde hair, and blue eyes. He tanned easily, although it was a farmer's tan. He never wore shorts, only wrangler jeans with boots. He loved to country-western dance, drink beer, watch the Dallas Cowboys play football, and the ladies. He was a true cowboy. He had worked on ranches. He had ridden broncs. We had met in our early twenties at our siblings' wedding (my brother married his sister). We were passionately attracted to each other from the moment we met. We married on December 29, 1990. We had our first son, Coy, in 1992, and our second son, J.R., was born in 1995.

We had a small ranch (seventy-five acres), raised cattle, and several horses. Our kids started rodeo at the age of five. Dean worked for the railroad (a career that followed my dad and grandfather). I taught school; I had completed my master's in education prior to our marrying.

Dean was a ladies' man. I often noticed when we went dancing or to a restaurant, ladies would look and flirt. He loved the attention. Once we were dancing at a Marie Osmond concert, Marie called out to the "cowboy in the white hat," took him up on stage, put her arm around his waist, and asked him to sing with her—a typical response to Dean.

Dean had *wild eyes*. I had a horse, a mare, named Milly. She often was quite temperamental. I could tell when I was saddling her what kind of ride it would be. Milly would get *wild eyes*. I knew if her eyes were wild that day, I better stay attentive, or I would get bucked off. Dean's eyes often had that same look, a look of unrest.

Dean had been a drinker since I met him. I had never been around alcoholism growing up and although I questioned if he could be an alcoholic, I rationalized his drinking pattern as just social behavior. I thought once Dean and I were married, the bar party life would end. Dean denied that he was an alcoholic. He claimed he could quit anytime, and several times throughout our marriage, Dean had quit drinking for periods of time. He had been arrested for DUI (driving under the influence) just a few years earlier. He had been ordered by the railroad to attend AA (Alcoholic Anonymous) meetings and to go to counseling. Dean would make comments how he did not have a problem like *those* people.

When we dated, we had built our entire relationship around going to the bar. In fact, I cannot recall any other date except dinner and then dancing at the bar. I claimed to be a Christian. I had grown up going to church, although I was not walking with the Lord. I was teaching school, finishing my masters' degree at the university, working as a cashier at Walmart on weekends, and living with a roommate in a small single-wide mobile home. I did not think Dean was a Christian, the Bible warns not to be "unequally yoked" (2 Corinthians 6:14). Dean reassured me that he was a believer. The Bible states, "You will know them by their fruits" (Matthew 7:16). Dean certainly did not display any godly fruit in his life. Upon reflection, I doubt I was displaying fruit either. I was out at the bar until early morning hours several nights a week and then late to work to teach school in the morning. I would turn off the classroom lights at lunch to sleep for thirty minutes on the floor before the kids came back into the room from lunch recess. I recently found a letter I had written to Dean when we dated. I am ashamed of the language I used in just casual writing and the attitude I portrayed. I was sleeping with Dean from early on in our dating, all the while holding on to a belief system that I was a good Christian girl. How could I have been so deceived and so blinded about who I was and so dismissal about my own sin?

For sixteen years, Dean and I had struggled in our marriage. I thought our married life would be different. I went to church weekly, took the kids to church, played the piano for church, taught Sunday school, got up early every morning, and did my devotionals with God. Somehow, in all the "good works," I believed I was walking with the Lord. There were certainly seasons where I was close to God, but there were also seasons where my sinful behavior had separated me from the Lord. Although, for years I thought I was a victim to my circumstances and a good Christian. Upon reflection, I certainly played a role in the demise of our marriage.

After one too many compromises, I wanted to end my life. I felt there was no way back to God. Dean had threatened that if I left him, he would tell people what I had done. I had sought the help of my pastor. He came out to the house and told us we needed to compromise in marriage. Dean would stop drinking if I did certain things; after all marriage was about compromise. To *save my marriage*, I had compromised to satisfy Dean, and he had not stopped drinking. Nowhere in the Bible does it state to compromise or that marriage is compromise. The Bible has a lot to say about marriage, and *compromise* is not a teaching of Jesus. In fact, John 14:15 states, "If you love me, you will keep my commandments," and James 4:17 states, "So whoever knows the right thing to do and fails to do it, for him it is sin." I no longer cared if people knew our dark secrets. I was determined that I was going to stop compromising and walk with the Lord. I pleaded for God to do whatever it took to save Dean.

There were so many nights that God came to my rescue. One night, when Dean was drunk, things escalated. I cannot remember what started the fight that night, and to be honest, I am not sure I even knew at the time. Dean was going for a gun. In desperation, I lifted my hands and cried out to God, "Binding Satan in the name of Jesus." Dean dropped to the floor. Literally, Dean, a 6'3" man, just fell to the floor. He was kicking and screaming and could not get up; it was as if God himself was holding him down. He lay there until finally he fell asleep. God showed up and protected us all that night. From that day on, Dean had fear; he would say that I had a *voodoo doll,* and I was sticking pins in it to hurt him. There was no *black magic.* God had chosen to intervene that night. God was not done rescuing my family and would continue to work miraculously.

Through the years, there had been multiple times I had suspected that Dean was cheating on me with other women. I would look through his pant pockets and wallet when he fell asleep. I heard rumors from other people. At one point, Dean stated, "Kath, you sure are dumb for an educated woman. I'm not giving up the girls. I want my cake and to eat it too." One night I heard Dean coming down the stairs on the phone. "I love you," he said into the phone. I proceeded to yell and questioned him. He got in the truck and drove to Colorado to meet up with the woman on the phone.

There is a story in the Bible about a woman named Leah. She too suffered rejection from her husband (Genesis 29). Her husband was named Jacob. Leah desired her husband to love her.

Jacob was in love with Laban's daughter Rachel. Jacob worked for Laban (served him) for seven years to have Rachel's hand in marriage. When his time of service was completed, Jacob stated, "Give me my wife, for my days are fulfilled, that I may go in to her" (Genesis 29:21). The Bible is so descriptive. I can't imagine Dean going to my dad and saying, "Let me marry Kath so I may go in to her." Laban planned the wedding, and Jacob was married, but Laban had tricked Jacob and given his oldest daughter, Leah, instead. I cannot understand how Jacob would not have realized that he had married Leah; he even consummated the marriage without realizing. Jacob must have consumed an ample supply of wine. When Jacob realized what happened, he questioned his father-in-law, Laban, "What is this you have done to me? Why have you deceived me" (Genesis 29:25)? Laban's response was simply: "It must not be done so in our country, to give the younger before the firstborn" (Genesis 29:26). Jacob arranged with Laban again to marry Rachel and worked an additional seven years. As a young girl, I was captivated by the love story of Jacob and Rachel. Jacob adored her. What kind of man would work (serve) fourteen years just to be able to marry the love of his life? Somehow, I had read (heard) that story numerous times and never saw Leah in the storyline, except that she had been given to Jacob through trickery. I wonder if Leah had anything to say in the situation. I can imagine the rejection, hurt, and horror when she realized that Jacob did not want her. If she had wanted to marry Jacob, it did not turn out as she had planned; Jacob did not love her. If she had not wanted to marry Jacob, she had been forced to enter a relationship with a man that did not want her. Rachel "envied her sister" (Genesis 30:1). She was stuck in a loveless marriage with a sister who hated and resented her.

Leah conceived and gave birth to a son, Reuben. She stated, "The Lord has surely looked on my affliction. Now therefore, my husband will love me" (Genesis 29:32). Then she conceived again and had another son, Simeon. This time she stated, "Because the Lord has heard that I am unloved, He has therefore given me this son also" (Genesis 29:33). She conceived again, gave birth to another son, and said, "Now this time my husband will become attached to me, because I have borne him three sons" (Genesis 29:34), and she named him Levi. Even after the fourth son, Judah, Leah did not win over the heart of Jacob.

I thought Dean would settle down after the birth of our first son, Coy. Then two years later, we had J.R. Even after having two boys, I did not have Dean's devoted love. I would later realize that without God, Dean did not even know how to love. I too erroneously believed that Dean would love me, quit drinking, and quit seeking others if only—if only we moved, if only we had kids, if only he got a different job, if only he had different friends, if only…

The day before Dean left for Colorado, my morning devotionals had been titled "Rock Bottom" (*Daily Bread*, August 19, 2005). The author had written, "My rock-bottom experience became a turning point and one of the most vital spiritual developments in my life." I had hit rock bottom. Dean never moved back home after that night; he stayed away for four days. Dean knew that I was miserable and wanted to commit suicide. He knew I wanted him out. He returned home to pack his things and decided to move to a town 270 miles away, where we had previously lived.

After two months of being separated, Dean told me about another woman he recently had met and slept with after a night at the bar. That encounter with her would change the course of his life.

Dean recalls that night even to this day. He got off a train about six in the evening. He looked south toward home then looked west toward the saloon (bar). He looked back south, then west. That evening, a voice deep inside told him to go home. He chose to go west and walked into the saloon. I thought the marriage separation would bring him to God. Dean was only further away from coming to Christ. I drove up to see him. I offered the opportunity to change his life and come home. He declined. He was depleting the bank account, partying, pursuing another woman, and enjoying the single life. I was physically ill from the stress. I was experiencing vertigo spells, emotionally drained, and financially sinking. After three months, I filed for divorce, and it was finalized in just a couple of weeks. Dean and I negotiated the paperwork together. I hired a lawyer just to help with the child custody portion and file the paperwork. The lawyer acted as a mediator on both of our behalf. We had met with him that morning. By evening, the lawyer called, "Ms. Tayler, congratulations! Your divorce is finalized." I did not even respond to him and hung up the phone. I walked into the bathroom, locked the door, sobbed uncontrollably, and vomited. After sixteen years, I had finally given up hope. No one in my family had ever gotten a divorce. I felt defeated and overwhelmed by the failure to save my marriage.

I was at a crossroads. I had made a conscious decision to leave my marriage, and now I had to give those memories to God. All those dark nights, all the secrets, all the hurt—I had to no longer own those memories. I went to God broken. I was ashamed of my own actions of compromise. I had no understanding of my identity in Christ. I felt worthless, rejected, and defeated. All these experiences had stolen my joy.

I could not recall the last time I had laughed, nor could I remember the last time I cried. Years of hurt had been bottled up, and now the tears would not stop flowing. There had been so many disappointments; however, I was sure that I had not shed a tear for over five years. Suppressing the hurt had also suppressed joy. When had I become a person so emotionally numb? I no longer wanted these memories—the memories of the kids hiding in the closet, me sneaking out with the kids to a hotel for the night, the compromises to try to keep things calm, the nights pretending I was asleep while I listened attentively to every move until he fell asleep. In all the trauma, all the dysfunction, I had lost myself. I poured myself into my career to escape feeling. I became a workaholic, filling every moment of my day. The drinking had destroyed him, me, and the kids. I could not bear to linger in those memories, so I poured my energy into work and graduate school.

I would not be able to keep the house. The bills were greater than my income. Dean was paying child support, but the amount was less than a tenth of his salary, far less than I was used to having to pay the household expenses. I struggled to buy groceries, put gas in the truck, and heat the house. My dad gave me a truckload of wood to help with the heating costs.

I knew people that had gone through divorce; they seemed happy. I had even heard that divorce will not hurt the kids; it is better for the kids to have happy parents than parents miserable in a marriage and fighting. However, I was finding that none of these belief systems were true. The kids were broken. I was broken. I struggled to find happiness in all the sadness that overwhelmed me. The Bible said to "pray without ceasing" and to "give thanks in all circumstances" (1 Thessalonians 5:16–17).

I sat down and made a list to count my blessings:

1. *I don't worry about Dean being drunk at night and coming up the stairs and emotionally abusing me or physically threatening me.*
2. *I know what income will come in, and it remains consistent. The money is far less, but I know what to expect.*
3. *I don't worry about Dean's unpredictable mood swings when he is drinking.*
4. *I don't have to compromise my faith!*
5. *I listen to Christian music in the house.*
6. *I have drawn closer to Christ.*
7. *I spend more time reading the Bible.*
8. *I don't have to drive the trash to town as often; I only have to take it once a week or less because it is not full of beer cans!*

Two months after the divorce, I did not feel better. I continued to struggle with the divorce. Everything was so overwhelming, and the unpredictable continued to happened. I had nightmares and would wake up crying and shaking. I clung to scriptures. "The Sovereign Lord will wipe away the tears from their faces" (Isaiah 25:8). I prayed without ceasing. I was exhausted and afraid to sleep at night because of the nightmares. In the day, I felt like I was living in a nightmare. One night, I read, "I am with you and will rescue you, declares the Lord" (Jeremiah 1:8). I prayed, "Rescue me, Lord." I sought God, clinging to the scriptures for comfort. I wrote in my prayer journal daily.

I am resisting letting go of Dean. I'm afraid of the unknown. I'm afraid of starting over. If I surrender, I may never get Dean back. I need to just give up on my will and say, "It is well with my soul." I may lose my house. Oh Lord, can you deal with my life? I cannot handle it. J.R. fell through the ceiling of the house. There is a huge hole in Coy's bedroom ceiling now, and it is cold and snowing outside. Thank you, God, that you protected him. Fix the ceiling please.

Three months had passed since the divorce was finalized. The kids were struggling. I called Dean; I would take him back if he would just give up the drinking and the girls. The kids had tried to call their dad for over a week, and he didn't answer the phone. They had not seen their dad in a month. He said he couldn't afford to take time off work. However, he had time to see the new girl he was dating and spent a week off with her traveling. I asked for an explanation. He responded, "She doesn't complain about my drinking. It's who I am." I wrote in my prayer journal that night.

Lord, why does all this still hurt so bad? He hasn't changed at all. God, please hear my plea; give me the strength to let him go.

I sought counseling. The counselor asked me to write down my goals and my greatest fears.

My goals in counseling:

1. *To identify my ex-marriage as toxic and be able to walk away—meaning, to let Dean go.*
2. *To decrease the nightmares.*

3. To receive skills to assist the kids in coping effectively with the divorce.
4. To be able to have contact with Dean and not be thrown into an emotional tailspin.
5. To allow myself the right to laugh and enjoy life.

My greatest fears:

1. The boys will never forgive me for the divorce. They will always regret their childhood. Permanent damage is done.
2. The boys will grow up and be drinkers.
3. I'll marry the wrong person and make a mistake again.
4. I won't be able to handle the home/ranch alone.
5. I'll always regret my life without Dean.

Six months passed. The counselor suggested I write a letter to Dean, one I would never mail. The task was to just get those feelings out. I was not making progress, whatever progress was supposed to be. I didn't know how to move on and get over it.

My dearest Dean,

You were so loving on the phone today. I miss you. My heart is still broken. There hasn't been a day yet that I don't break down and cry. My counselor thinks I should consider antidepressants.

I remember your sober days. Those days I miss. I miss the way we would make love. I thought it was always just sex to you. But you told me today you miss making love to me.

I wanted to beg you on the phone to come home. The boys need you. I need you. All of us are hurting so bad.

I feel like you're Dr. Jerkel and Mr. Hyde. One day, you're so wonderful. The next, you are justifying your drinking and talking about your "right to flirt."

*You would get so mad when I told you I see
your potential. I still cling to that fantasy.
It's been six months. and I'm still falling apart.*

Kath

Dean came that weekend to pick up farm and ranch equipment from the house. He told me he loved me still; it even looked like there were tears in his eyes, although he denied it. I told him the offer still stood: "Give up the drinking and the girls." He answered, "It's better we're apart." That weekend was extremely hard on me. I felt exhausted and sick. I went to bed. I got up on Sunday to go to church and decided I didn't have the strength and just went back to bed. Every time I saw or spoke with Dean, I was an emotional wreck.

I went to an AA meeting and bought books about codependents. I tried to understand Dean's drinking. One of the guys there told me, "Don't take your ex-husband's drinking personally. It has nothing to do with you." He gave me a copy of the *Serenity Prayer*.

"O God and Heavenly Father grant to us the serenity of mind to accept that which cannot be changed, courage to change that which can be changed, and wisdom to know the one from the other through Jesus Christ, our Lord, Amen" (Niebuhr 1930).

I prayed that prayer daily. I worried constantly about the boys. The boys would go spend time at Dean's place on the weekends, school breaks, or the summer. I was miserable without the kids. I was fearful the entire time the kids were away. Dean was often gone, out of town for work on a train, and the boys were completely alone. Often, Dean was drinking, and I wasn't there to intervene. That summer, Dean was gone, and the boys were involved in a rollover on the four-wheeler. Thank God, although injured, they were both okay. I rushed to see the boys. His place was three and half hours away and all on back country roads, no interstate. Before I left his place that evening, I offered Dean the chance to have his family back again. A full year had passed since he left that night for Colorado, and we separated. He replied, "I'll never walk the line," a line from a country song by Johnny Cash. That day was the last time I offered Dean reconciliation. I shut the door. I went home that night and prayed, "Today, Lord, I let go. God, he is yours. Save Dean. Do whatever it takes, but he is yours, Lord."

I wrote in my prayer journal a portion from a song I had heard.

> *Just as I am*
> *I come broken to be mended*
> *I come wounded to be healed*
> *I come desperate to be rescued*
> *I come empty to be filled*
> *I come broken, Just as I am! (Cottrell)*

I was worried about the kids. I felt Dean could not be a responsible parent. His drinking and absenteeism put the kids in unsafe situations. Coy told me he had driven Dad and his little brother, J.R., home from a nearby town, a total of twenty-five miles at night. Dean had been drinking, and Coy was only fourteen years old and did not have a driver's license. Coy had driven the truck on the ranch since a young age. I would stand in the back off the truck and throw hay to the cattle as he drove. Although, in no way did Coy have the experience to drive on public roads. I decided to seek a lawyer and go after full custody of the boys. I knew Dean would fight me for them. I knew the boys would be furious at me and disagree with my decision. I prayed God would intervene.

Less than four months later, Dean was sitting in a jail cell. How could I have possibly known that my prayer, "Lord, do whatever it takes to save Dean," was beginning to be fulfilled? Years would pass before I would see what God was doing. I was beginning my own journey, one that would be filled with mistakes, regrets, healing, and restoration.

CHAPTER 3

A Single Mom

I sat on the stairs, reading the letter Dean had sent to his parents. His explanation of the events around that night disgusted me. I felt as if I was going to vomit. I had taken the kids to see their grandparents, Dean's parents. They lived 250 miles away from our home. "See, it is not his fault," said his mom. Nothing was ever Dean's fault. The divorce certainly was not his fault. "There's two sides to every story," his mom would say. The drinking was not Dean's fault; he did not have a drinking problem. Now this, and it was someone else's fault. I was still reading the letter when the phone rang.

His mom said the phone call was for me. Dean was on the phone. I felt like his mom, and Dean had planned for him to call when I was there. He was calling from jail. The conversation was being recorded, and we had 10 minutes to talk. I had not spoken to Dean since his arrest. His arrest had been weeks prior. I reluctantly took the phone and walked up to the top of the stairs, sitting down on the top step. "Kath, I'm going to make this up to you," Dean stated. He believed he would be out of jail soon. He was really changing this time. "I've 'accepted Jesus,'" he stated. He was going to come home, and everything was going to be all right. I sat listening, puzzled at Dean's audacity. I doubted Dean would *get off* these charges. Regardless of the outcome, him coming home was not something I was willing to even consider. There was no way in my mind that Dean could make up anything to me. He had bargained with God before with his previous DUI (driving under the influence charge), and I believed this was one of those pleads: "If you get me off this time, God, I'll give you my life"—all things I had heard before.

I got off the phone and walked back down the stairs. Dean's mom was waiting for me. "See," she said, "It's not his fault." His parents had Dean's belongings; Dean was putting them as *power of attorney* during this ordeal. I asked his parents for the boys' items, the truck, and trailer. "I'll need to sell the truck and trailer to be able to pay the mortgage since child support just stopped." His mom refused to release anything. "Dean will be out and come home. Those are his things. We will need the truck and trailer to move his things here," she said.

Against the advice of friends and family, I wrote Dean in jail.

January 6, 2007

Dean,

When we got separated and then divorced, I wrote you letters... dozens of them. However, I never mailed them. My counselor felt that I should refrain from sending them and only use them to heal. Since the news on December 10th, I can't sleep, and my mind races with everything. Against the advice of family and friends, I'm writing to you. Those who love me tell me to stay quiet, but I have never really told you all I need to say. I promise you that this letter will be very difficult to read and will impact you forever. I am leaving you to decide if you are in the emotional state to handle its content. If you feel that you are not able to read it, then put it away.

Before you put this letter down let, me begin with the financial stuff, not because it is more important than the rest of the letter but because if you stop reading, I have at least communicated with you. When we got off the phone, I told your parents

I needed the vehicle titles. Your mom became very defensive that they need the truck to move you out. I said, "Of course." However, throughout the course of the day, the kids asked for different things that were their belongings, and your mom said, "No." She is guarding the items and is very defensive that I'm after your stuff. I'm trying hard not to be bitter. Until a year ago, those items were also mine. I've worked my whole life and have been more than generous in the divorce and the division of property. The kids stand in line with me to get discounted food (sometimes we stand in line for over two hours). We are losing our home. I lost my entire December check to immediately add the kids to health insurance. I disconnected the TV, the phone, and the Internet. We turned down the heat and burn fires in the wood stove. Coy swears when he turns 15 this summer, he will get a job and help me with the bills. You may be thinking this is trivial while you are in jail; but, Dean, these are your children, and I'm doing the best I can financially.

I have read the articles in the newspapers and watched the story on the news on TV. They have quoted the 911 call and the statements you initially gave the police. I will try not to approach the content of the case. What I believe is really irrelevant at this time. I read the letter you wrote to your mom and dad. If your intent was to convince your mom of your innocence and how you are being framed, you were successful.

As you recall, when our marriage was crumbling, I went to the doctor for tranquillizers... I too had suicidal tendencies. I am ashamed of the extremes I took to save our marriage and make you happy. I have humbly asked God for forgiveness and began a new life. Currently, the boys don't know anything about this content, and I would love to protect them from any more hurt.

I cannot begin to tell you how many lives were impacted by the event that occurred on December 10th. The kids took off school a day, and I stayed home from work on that following Monday. By 4:00 in the afternoon, the boys were receiving text messages. The phone began to ring off the hook. The boys didn't want to ever go back to school. They returned to school to hear the whispers in the hall about their dad. They came home each afternoon in shambles. And I couldn't take the hurt away. The words on this page cannot begin to show you the devastation and the hurt. No child should ever have to go through what the boys have endured. I returned to work on Tuesday to find it had spread through campus like a wildfire. We all hung our heads in shame.

Your letter to us said that when you "live your life on the line, bad things happen, even if you don't do bad things." Forgive me if my accusations are incorrect, you did do "bad" things. Perhaps my memory is different from yours. I remember you mixing prescription drugs with alcohol and how dangerous you would become. I remember stuff only to have you say it wasn't your fault. You didn't ever remember it; after all you were on drugs and alcohol. I remember you having no guilt for your activities, your numerous conversations that it wasn't sin, and never once apologizing only excuses or exact question games. You thought I was so ignorant that I didn't know how you behaved when away from me. I remember begging you to "get your life right and come home." But as you told me, "I'll never walk the line." According to you, "life is supposed to be fun." I remember calling your dad and telling him I was afraid of you, and

I needed to be able to go to bed at night and not be afraid of you coming up the stairs drunk.

Over the holidays, your sister said that you wanted to "get back together and come home," but I wouldn't meet you halfway. She believed that I wouldn't move, causing us to be divorced. That statement is so far from the truth. We are not together because you never had a "heart" change. I would have to accept alcoholism and sexual immortality. You never believed you had a drinking problem (probably still don't). Do you remember what you told me before I filed for divorce? I do, it's burned in my memory. I say that phrase almost every day in my mind. "Kath, for someone working on her doctorate, you are pretty dumb. I haven't stopped drinking for 15 years, so it's a pretty good bet that I'm not going to stop." In your letter you said, "I couldn't be a good husband." Accept the responsibility, Dean. You chose not to be a good husband.

I believe you can get out of prison the same man you were before you went in. To be frank, our children deserve better. Our children deserve a man of character and integrity, a man that has a heart for God and his family. Even from prison, you can become a man of character. Your influence with those boys is great. You can choose to teach the ways of God, repentance, and integrity, or you can choose to take a different path. The choice is yours.

You stated on the phone and in the letter that if you get out, you're going to "make it up to us." I don't know if you knew that you had a wife and kids that truly loved you. When you were in jail before, you bargained with God. You promised me and God the drinking was over. When we got divorced, you promised you would not drink when you had the children. Of course, I am aware of your drinking when the children were with you. I will not stand idly by and let you return to your life and put our children in danger.

I believe life is full of "defining" moments. Those moments define your life forever. This is your defining moment. What kind of man will you become? What path will you choose? Are your promises empty, or do you mean it this time?

Kathleen

January 26, 2007

Dean,

I cannot answer all your questions. I can only tell you that God has spoken to me most of my life. There was a time though, that God fell silent. Do you remember when I told you that our marriage was pulling me further away from God? The more I sinned, the more we were in involved in ungodly activity, the more He was silent. I had not heard God for several years until we separated. God needed me removed from our marriage to restore my relationship completely with Him. He also needed me removed to finely reach you. There are scriptures in the Bible that reference how as humans we must confess sin and turn from sin to hear His voice; thus, I think the reason that when I used to tell the kids that they could hear God you used to say that you had never heard him. Ask God to reveal to you what you need to confess or do to have communication with him. He will reveal to you what is blocking that communication, be honest with yourself, him, and others. God's relationship with each person is different. As I told you, I knew something occurred at 2:00 a.m. that morning. I regret that although God speaks with me, I can stop or change things. I know that God will communicate with you through prayer time, worship, and reading His word. By the time you receive this letter, your prayer-fast will be over. I hope you found the answers you were looking for from God.

The kids got your letters two days ago. Coy went into his room and cried and cried. He never talked to me about it. Coy must "heal" and that is going to take God and time.

We have had tons of snow and ice storms. The trees broke a lot from all the weight. I had wrapped the pipes outside in insulation (I learned my lesson after that one broke last year); however, I still had a pipe bust. I've had the water off for a week outside. Hopefully today I can finally get out there and fix it with Coy.

In all of this heartache, I have learned that God is all I need. I've lost so much...you, the horses, and the house. In all the hurt though, God has blessed me and is providing. I think of all I lost, and then I realize how much more you have lost. Dean, I want you to know that I do forgive you. I often wish that things could have been different. I couldn't let you go until now; but finally, God has freed me. Now that I know God has you, I can finally release you to him. I was such a "codependent" always trying to take care of you and obviously I didn't do a very good job. I had a "false God" too Dean, I honestly put you above God for years. I'm glad that you are seeking Him. When you lose everything, God is all you need. When you are at the bottom, God will rise you up.

Keep the kids in your prayers Dean. I cannot begin to tell you how much they are both struggling emotionally. I don't think they will ever "get over" all of this, but they can reach a place of peace and forgiveness. Dean, we can't change the past; But we can choose to change our future by seeking God daily.

Kath

January 30, 2007

Dear Dean,

I was waiting to mail this letter for Coy and J.R. to write. J.R.'s letter is enclosed. Coy did not write. A family member called me recently and asked if I keep the kids from seeing your letters, if I keep the kids from writing and blocked my phone. All the rumors!!! Life is hard enough on us!!! I'm the one that encouraged you to write them. I ask the kids every time I mail to you if they want to put a letter in. Unfortunately, Coy is not at that place where he is willing to write. Dean, he is really hurting. Until you wrote to him personally, Coy refused to listen to any of the letters I received. J.R. asked me to read the first letter to him (the one Kathleen and the boys), and Coy walked out of the room. I did not block the phone, I have no idea what that is about; however, if you called collect, I couldn't afford it. We are really struggling financially.

We heard rumors that you have another hearing in 2–4 weeks. Should you get out on bail, you can see the kids if they want to see you, but you won't have custody. You need time to change. I don't hate you. I'm not after revenge, but I need the kids to be safe. You would never intentionally hurt them, but the lifestyle you were living put them at risk. Please try to understand.

I know God has you now. Kathleen

Bail was never granted for Dean. His trial was six months later. The district attorney called and said the court was considering issuing a subpoena for my appearance. They wanted me to testify to Dean's drinking behavior from the past. I wrote Dean, begging him to keep the kids and me from being called into court. Dean succeeded, and we did not have to appear. Upon request, I submitted a written statement to the court. That statement would not influence the court's decision on sentencing; however, it caused harm emotionally to Dean. Years later, Dean would still mention that statement, and the wound was deep. My parents obtained the cassette tapes from the trial. We listened to the trial. The boys and I did not attend the trial. I felt it was more than I could bear. The following October 2007, Dean was sitting in prison with a sixteen-year sentence. (Originally, the district attorney had pursued thirty years.) Often, going to trial can take years. Dean received his sentence just seven months after that tragic December night.

His mom and dad never let us get those things. For years, I was bitter that they kept everything. I understand now that she truly believed he would get out any day and come home. They no longer called or interacted with me and the boys. My brother was married to Dean's sister. They too withdrew, and we had little to no interaction with them. They had children. The boys lost interaction with their cousins. That day, the boys lost their dad, their grandparents, their cousins, and their aunt and uncle. Unfortunately, it was just the beginning of everything they would lose that year.

Coy lost his horse. He was yelling when he came running into the house. "Mom! Mom! I can't find Cody." He would sing to her. I called him the horse whisperer. I could feel the pit in my stomach. His mare was too old to run away, almost thirty years old, which was old for a horse. I went out and walked the pasture. She was down and thrashing. I needed to put her out of her misery. I just could not shoot her, and Coy was the best shot. But she was his horse, and he was just a kid. I made some phone calls, and a friend of a friend showed up at the door with his rifle in hand. "Ma'am, Mr. Chavez called me."

As he proceeded to the pasture, the boys and I huddled in the house, crying. "Oh, Lord, please help us," I whispered.

The man shot her and returned to the house. "I'm so sorry, ma'am. Is there anything I can do for you?" he asked. He proceeded to invite us to church.

I told him we had a local church and thanked him for his time. I called the livestock removal company to come pick up the horse. I had to turn away and choke back the tears as they loaded the dead horse's body.

That same year, Coy's dog, Felony, would die. Coy insisted I bury her. I had never buried anything and was going to transport her to the local vet for disposal. Coy insisted that she be buried on the ranch. The ground was hard and dry, like rock. I sat outside, crying to God, "How am I supposed to bury this dog deep enough that the coyotes don't dig her up?" I called my mom, who advised me to turn on the water hose and let it run a while to soften the dirt. I finally dug what I thought was enough and gently pushed the dog into the grave. The hole was too shallow. I continued to dig for hours, with tears running down my face. Eventually, the grave was finished. I constructed a small cross out of twigs and string and put it on top of the mound.

That evening, J.R. walked into the kitchen when I was cooking dinner. "Mom, you said that God never gives us more than we can handle." J.R. was only in the seventh grade.

"Yes, that is true," I replied.

J.R. then stated, "Mom, you said that with God, all things are possible."

"Yes," I nodded.

J.R. looked exasperated, "Then there is no end to all of this because with God we can handle everything!" He walked out of the kitchen as I stood, overwhelmed with his statement.

"Surely, Lord, there is an end to this all," I prayed.

Coy struggled with his stomach that year. We went to several doctors. His attendance at school was poor. His grades were declining. The school called a meeting. I recall sitting in that meeting, listening to one high-school English teacher. "He doesn't care. He doesn't do his homework." She proceeded to go on, "I don't think anyone is helping him at home." Her accusations were brutal, missing any compassion or understanding for Coy. I had been a teacher myself for fifteen-plus years and certainly understood the concern; however, I felt as if there was no understanding for the situation Coy had endured and the multiple factors that were contributing to his academic and emotional decline.

I had vertigo spells for the first time in my life. I recall going to several doctors and many replying, "So you're having dizzy spells." Dizziness and vertigo are not the same. Obviously, these doctors had never experienced vertigo. Vertigo was like sitting in the teacup ride at an amusement park and spinning so fast that one cannot focus on anything and has no idea what is up or down. Stress was affecting all of us and our physical health was bearing the strain. I was physically sick all the time.

J.R. withdrew and became a huge introvert. Teachers would comment that he never spoke in school. He wrote music and would sing with his guitar. He wrote the lyrics, "I had a life that I remember, my whole family had each other. Then one day, all of that changed. My mother and my father got separated. We all moved on, but sometimes I cry. We will be better someday." J.R. would pray for his dad and tell me often, "Someday dad is going to come home. You guys will get back together. Dad is going to accept Jesus and change." J.R. held on to that hope and continued to pray for his dad. I had given up.

The house was up for sale. We would eventually sell all the livestock, even the kids' rodeo horses. I was teaching at a university, juggling the boys' basketball games, and working side-contract work. The boys became "latchkey" kids, home alone much of the time. Dean's choices had cost us all so much. I was angry and blamed everything on him.

The band Casting Crowns just released a song, "I'll Praise You in This Storm." The words stated, "I was sure, by now, God, you would have reached down and wiped our tears away, stepped in, and saved the day. But once again, I say amen, and it's still raining. As the thunder rolls, I barely hear your whisper through the rain, 'I'm with you.' And as your mercy falls, I raise my hands and praise the God who gives and takes away" (Beach Street Records 2005). I went outside and drew a line in the dirt. A huge storm was blowing in, the wind was howling. I raised my hands and shouted, "I will praise you in this storm!" Tears were streaming down my face. I listened to that song every day for six months. I wondered if God saw us, although I could feel his close presence each night when I crawled into bed. At times, it felt as if God's arms were around me. In later years, I would miss that feeling of God hugging me. God knew at that time I could not manage without his presence in a very tangible way.

There is a poem called "Footprints in the Sand." In the poem, the writer looks at footprints on a beach and notices that during his hardest times in life, there was only one set of prints. Although, at other times, he could see his footprints and the footprints of Christ. So he asked God why in the hardest times did God abandon him and not walk by his side. God responded, "In those times, I carried you." God would carry me through that year. Many days would become a blur as I functioned day by day in survival stage. Joshua 1:5 states, "As I was with Moses, so I will be with you; I will never leave you nor forsake you." God was not leaving me, and I relied on him day by day, and sometimes moment by moment, to get me through.

I looked for homes in town; everything seemed above our price range. I could not find anything to rent that was in our price range and would allow dogs. Buying was the only option. When I showed real estate photos of what we could afford to Coy and J.R., they argued that they were not going to live there and why we had to let go of our home. They had already lost so much; we all had.

I considered moving closer to my parents. I was sinking financially, and we did not live in town with any family. The nearest family was 230 miles away. Coy and J.R. were already so upset in losing so much and argued they did not want to change schools and lose their friends. Both boys played on the school basketball team and at that time were also playing football. I had to find a way where the boys could finish high school at their current school. I remember one day, J.R. had a basketball game out of town after school. The bus would not be back until around 11:00 p.m. J.R. asked for some money so he could buy some dinner on the road. The bank account was down to $1.68. Over fifteen years has passed, and I still remember the exact amount. The refrigerator was empty, the bank account was empty, and J.R. would go out of town to his game without being able to eat. The local church in town had a food shipment come to town once a month; an entire box of food could be purchased for $50. I would pick up a box once a month, sometimes waiting in line for hours. There was never any beef, but there was chicken. There was canned milk, cereal, and some canned vegetables. We couldn't choose the food, but at least we could eat. To this day, the boys are not fond of chicken; they claim it was all we ate. I still feel that pit in my stomach as I recall those days.

I remember once, when we were traveling, I pulled through a fast-food restaurant to get the boys something to eat. I didn't have enough money for all of us. I just ordered food for the boys. Coy asked, "Mom, aren't you going to eat." I responded, "I'm not hungry." I know Coy knew that we didn't have enough money. He said, "Hey, Mom, how about we share my hamburger." I still get tears in my eyes remembering that day and his compassion.

After payday, I asked J.R. to go into the cafeteria at school and ask how much I owed. J.R. came home and said, "Mrs. Craig said we don't owe anything." I was sure it was a misunderstanding. I called the school to settle my cafeteria bill; they repeated what J.R. had been told, "Your account is paid, Mrs. Tayler." Someone paid for my boys' lunches for the rest of the year. I told the school my bill was not paid, but they just repeated my account was fine. They never said someone paid, but I knew someone must have paid.

When it was time for basketball shoes, I told J.R. I would have to buy a cheaper pair at the local sports shop instead of the team shoes, which were $100 a pair. J.R. said the coach ordered his shoes and coach said would pay for them.

At Christmas, both boys needed a winter coat. I explained that I could not buy other things because we just did not have the money. They understood. At work, the college of education was hosting a book fair to raise funds. I "randomly" won a "drawing" for $100 of free books from the Scholastic Book Fair. I was able to get books for the boys to have a Christmas gift. Coy loved Gary Paulsen survival books (especially *Hatchet*), and J.R. was into the series *A Tale of Unfortunate Events* (Snicket and Helquist 1999). J.R. was already on the third book of the series when he begged me to read them with him. He stated we should start at the first book, even though he had already finished the first two. At the end of the first book, I told J.R., "These books are horrible. Everything goes wrong. It better get better in the second book."

J.R. responded that "It does not get better."

I inquired, "Why do you like these books?"

I still remember his answer, "Because, Mom, they have it worse than we do." Thus, we continued to read several more of books in the series.

The boys and I did not talk about the situation at their school or at my work, but God placed people in our lives that helped anonymously. To this day, I do not know who paid that lunch bill or did those other acts of kindness. On paper, there was no way I could make the monthly bills due; however, somehow, we continued to make it month to month. God was providing for us.

I read the words written again and again, "A father to the fatherless, and a judge of the widows" (Psalm 68:5). God is the father to the fatherless; he defends the widow. I certainly understood that I was not a widow, but there were similarities. I was without any support emotionally, spiritually, and financially. The boys had a father but now were being raised with an absent father. Even though Dean would call them occasionally from the prison and there were occasional letters addressed to them, there was not an active father in their lives. The words of the scripture rooted deep within my soul. "Father," I prayed, "Be the father to my boys." That simple prayer would be mouthed thousands of times over the years that followed.

I considered dropping out of the doctoral program. I had signed a contract in which my doctoral scholarship was tied to my employment. I would have to look for a job, which might be difficult to obtain since it was midyear. Finding a job in August would be much easier than December for a teacher. Coy stated, "Mom, I can help. Don't give up on your dreams." He would step up and manage things when I was away at school or work. At one point, I thought Coy was too young to assume so much responsibility and hired a "live-in nanny." Sarah was a local college student and received room and board in exchange for watching the boys when I was teaching nights or attending school at night. She would also pick the boys up from basketball practice and get them to games. She became part of the family. I felt like Coy had to grow up too fast. He would help me to do numerous home repairs: replace broken water pipes, lay tile in the bathroom, replace the leaking toilet seal, replace electrical outlets, and fix shingles on the roof.

Coy felt responsible for not being at his dad's that December night; somehow, he thought the outcome would have been different if he had been there. At one point, I took off work and went to classes with him at high school; his grades were suffering. I told him, if he couldn't show up to class and do his work, then I would go with him. He lost phone and extracurricular privileges. He dropped weight and decided he was a "vegetarian" but hated vegetables, which translated to not eating anything or very little. I was determined to fight for him since he appeared to have no fight left.

One day, I walked out to the old shed to make sure the barn cats had food. I swung open the door. There, in the middle of the shed, hung a rope noose from the center rafter. My legs gave out under me as I fell to the dirt floor. I cried and screamed out to God. I was thankful that the noose was empty but was overwhelmed that someone had hung it there. I went out to the barn and got the ladder. I proceeded up the ladder and, with a pocketknife, sawed the noose down. I went around the barn, the tack room, the boys' room, and gathered every rope on the place. I questioned the boys when they got home from school. To this day, no one has ever confessed to the hanging that noose.

The boys had a close friend, C.J. He was in between both boys in age. C.J.'s mom had left his dad and moved away out of state. They had been having marriage difficulties for years, and she had finally given up. His dad often drank alcohol and was often mean. His dad kicked him out of the house, pinning him up against a pickup and telling him that he could no longer live there. C.J.'s dad had moved in his girlfriend, and she was not fond of C.J. She had her own kids to move into the house. C.J. came over to the house and said he did not know what he was going to do. We brought in an extra mattress from the garage and laid it on the floor of the boys' room. From that moment, C.J. became my son and lived with us on and off for several years.

The boys were angry at the choices their dad made with alcoholism. However, two of the three boys would struggle with drinking too much in future years. One of the boys was out drinking with several other basketball players from their high school, driving on a backcountry dirt road he rolled the pickup and was pinned inside. Somehow, he managed to call 911. The basketball kids had all run away and left my son pinned inside; the other boys were fearful of being caught by the police. One of the coaches of the team had purchased the alcohol for the boys, which later was verified by the convenience store videotape footage. Later in life, that same son would incur another DUI (driving under the influence) and call me from a jail cell in Texas. He would be court mandated to install a Breathalyzer on his vehicle. He hated the choices his dad made with alcohol, but he was repeating the same pattern. Another son would consume too much alcohol regularly; his girlfriend/fiancée (now his wife) called me and asked me to intervene. I picked him up in the car and went out for a drive. I yelled and scolded him about his choices and the path he was taking. Both boys would continue to engage in drinking too much alcohol through adulthood. Statistics state that over half of children raised with a parent engaging in substance abuse will show evidence of alcohol or drug use by young adulthood. My boys were becoming another statistic.

I was relieved that my other son did not seem interested in alcohol, although I had found a bottle of hard liquor in his closet at one point. To my shock, he was arrested and charged for having drug paraphernalia (marijuana and a pipe) when stopped by traffic police. He was over eighteen years old at the time, so he would successfully hide the event from me for months. He would have to appear in court, serve probation, have random drug testing, and upon completion of probation (without further events) could have his court record sealed. He was a senior in high school, had dropped off the basketball team, and was struggling.

Occasionally, through the years, I would write Dean updates on the boys and send photos of them. I would send newspaper clippings of their sports events, graduation announcements, or other updates. I blamed him for the boys' choices and their struggles. At one point, Dean wrote back.

9/6/2013

Dear Kath,

I appreciate the photos as well as the update on the boys. I had no idea about the troubles; it really caught me off guard. Not in my wildest dreams would I have guessed they would be using. Kath, this scares me. The only place drugs and alcohol lead is prison or the graveyard. I always thought me coming to prison was of course for my salvation, but the greater good coming from it was to get me out of the boys' lives because I was leading them to where I'm now. It really sucks that they haven't learned from my mistakes. Again, I'm so sorry I'm not there to help.

Dean

I required that if the boys lived in my home, they would attend church with me on Sundays. I would drag them to church, but I could not make them *drink the water*. I prayed that they were listening to the pastor's message, that seeds were being planted, that God was reaching their hearts. I pleaded with God to protect my boys from becoming one of the statistics. Approximately five million kids, before the age of eighteen, will have a parent incarcerated during their childhood years (US census 2022). Many of these children do time themselves behind prison walls as adults. I had read numerous studies; I knew what the statistics stated and knew their possible fate. I wanted more for them. I battled in prayer that God would be their Father, that he would raise them, that he would protect them, and that he would help them to make good choices. I was failing miserably. How did God expect me to raise the boys alone?

I wanted a man to come rescue me and the boys. There is a story in the Bible about a woman named Ruth. I always loved that story, even as a little girl. Ruth's husband died. In biblical times, if a woman lost her husband to death, then the brother of the husband is to marry the woman. However, Ruth's husband's brother was also dead. Her father-in-law had also died.

Ruth left with her mother-in-law (Naomi) to the land of Judah. There she met an attractive landowner, Boaz. He was a relative of Naomi's dead husband. Ruth gathered grain in Boaz's fields after the reapers (workers). Boaz noticed Ruth and gave her favor. He told his workers to leave grain for her, not to touch her and give her water as she needed. Ruth pursued Boaz by waiting until he was asleep, removing the blanket off his feet, and lying down at his feet. Boaz woke up and found Ruth there. He inquired what she was doing there, and her response was, "I am Ruth, your servant. Spread your wings over your servant, for you are a redeemer" (Ruth 3:9). Boaz and Ruth married. Their union became part of the direct family line, geology of Jesus. I prayed for a man to come be my redeemer, my Boaz. Thus, that mindset would cause me so much harm. Through tears and heartbreak, I would continue to learn only God could be my redeemer.

CHAPTER 4

The Wolf in Sheep's Clothing

I felt rejected and alone. I wanted to be loved. I wish I would have trusted God for his provision, but I worried about financially providing. I met a man (Leslie) at church. He appeared sincere, although now, in reflection, there were red flags that I chose to dismiss. Leslie had been married four times previously. I thought I was in love, but honestly, I was in hurt and rebound. Leslie offered us a home and financial security. I thought this man was the answer to all our problems. We married that year. Instead of clinging to God to fill that emptiness and for provision, I sought a man. Leslie was destructive; he lived a double life: one life at church and work, and a totally different life at home. He struggled with sexual addiction, unmedicated mental illness, and manic episodes. Leslie was infatuated with inappropriate idealization of young men and engaged in pornography in that realm. He sought inappropriate attention from males and females. I feared for my adolescent boys. I had put myself and my boys in harm's way. Matthew 7:15 states, "Beware of false prophets, who come to you in sheep's clothing, but inwardly they are ravening wolves." He was a wolf hanging out in church and preying on wounded women.

One evening, in a manic episode, he called 911. At the time, my son Coy was working as a 911 operator. Leslie did not even recognize Coy's voice. Leslie yelled that he was barricaded in a bedroom and that a woman had a gun and was going to kill him. I could hear

Leslie on the phone through the barricaded door. I was trying to reason with him, but he was in an episode again, and the voices in his head were louder than my voice. Coy had to dispatch the police. The police came running into our home and had me up against the wall with my arms and legs spread. Leslie proceeded to tell the police that it was his house, and I was an intruder. I explained to the police that I was his wife. I had to find our marriage certificate to show the police. Furthermore, I did not even know the combination to unlock the gun cabinet. That gun case was Coy's, and he stored his guns in there. I called a pastor who also worked as the police chaplain. He immediately came over and validated my story. The police asked me if Leslie was off his meds. I had never seen Leslie take medicine. When I had questioned Leslie previously about mental illness, he became outraged and denied any allegations. Coy moved out that night when he got off work. I am sure he was embarrassed at work by the whole situation. Coy could no longer deal with the instability and drama at home.

I found a Christian counseling center that specialized in sexual addictions in Colorado. Leslie agreed to go for an intensive week with me and then to continue counseling/treatment via distance for the next several months. The counselor met with me alone. He told me Leslie was a narcissist, had mental illness, doubted his claims of Christianity, and was less than optimistic about Leslie's prognosis for recovery. I had never heard the word *narcissist*, even though I had obtained a degree in psychology twenty years prior. I researched the characteristics and agreed that Leslie did act like the world revolved around him, and he had excessive admiration of himself. Furthermore, the counselor felt that Leslie has mental illness, and further evaluation was warranted. I knew Leslie had a formal mental diagnosis but never did disclose to me the findings. I worried about schizophrenia. Leslie often heard voices and would act on those voices. I would be advised on multiple occasions that for my own safety and the boys', to leave the relationship.

Leslie would get up late at night and sneak out to the living room to get on his computer and the Internet. He would engage in immoral activities. One night, I saw the silhouette of a large, black, monstrous shape standing at our bedroom door. I turned to Leslie and stated, "He is waiting for you."

Leslie inquired, "Who?"

I responded, "I can see the demon and feel the evil. Don't leave him waiting. Go ahead."

Needless to say, Leslie did not proceed to get up that night and leave the bedroom. The reality was, I was not joking; I would see the demon and feel the evil in our home. At one point, even J.R. commented that he saw demons one night in his room. I had never discussed with J.R. seeing the demon or feeling the evil spirits prior to his comment. I would anoint the home with oil and pray.

I searched through old files stored in the garage and found state mental institution commitment papers on Leslie; he had been committed to a state mental institution. The state has civil commitment laws in which individual with severe mental illness can be involuntarily committed. There were also papers of allegations of him found in the institution in a bed of a minor male. There were accusations filed in the court. There were documents in which he was the number one suspect in a missing persons investigation of a woman jogger. His behavior and these documents of previous events scared me. I located all four of his ex-wives, and they all told similar stories of his behavior and events that had occurred. Two of the previous ex-wives had feared for their lives.

I picked up the divorce packet from the county courthouse. I self-represented, even though Leslie hired a lawyer on retainer. Leslie and I divorced. The boys and I left the house with just the things we had moved in with, leaving most of the furniture and even the dishes. Leslie took the house and my truck, a truck I had paid for prior to our marrying. I refused to fight. I just wanted out. Later I heard that Leslie told people in town I hired a big lawyer from the city and "took him to the cleaners." I did not even comment back on the rumors. I knew the truth.

My choice had caused more hurt for my boys and me. I can justify that it was not my fault; however, I knew that my own choice and sin had put us in this circumstance. I chose to not wait on God. I chose to get involved when there had clearly been red flags. I chose to fill the hole in my heart with a man instead of Christ. To pretend that my sin did not put us in that situation or that I had no responsibility would be untruthful. I paid dearly for that choice, and so did my boys. Of my regrets in life, this one would certainly be at the top. Since our divorce, Leslie has married and divorced several more times. I pray God would stop his cycle of destruction.

My self-esteem had crashed; I felt rejected and even more damaged. I struggled with depression. I sought medical help to deal with anxiety and depression. I continued in Christian counseling. Ephesians 2:4–8 states, "But God, who is rich in mercy because of His great love with which He loved us, even when we were dead in trespasses, made us alive together with Christ (by grace you have been saved), and raised us up together, and made us sit together in the heavenly places in Christ Jesus, that in the ages to come He might show the exceeding riches of His grace in His kindness towards us in Christ Jesus. For by grace, you have been saved through faith, and that not of yourselves; it is a gift of God." *But God*—those two words change everything. God began to heal me and work with me to find my identity in Christ.

I clung to Jeremiah 29:11: "For I know the thoughts that I think towards you, says the Lord, thoughts of peace and not of evil, to give you a future and a hope." I put the words up across the wall in our home. I had the verse on my key chain. God had a plan for my life. By his grace and his grace alone, I was forgiven. He had a plan for my life and my boys.

I was reminded of the story of the *woman at the well* (John 4). Her past was full of bad choices, multiple failed marriages (five to be exact), and was currently living with a man who was not her husband. She felt unloved, unworthy, damaged, and unclean. I can image that she felt rejected, condemned, and beyond hope. On that day, the Samaritan woman took the journey to *Jacob's well* in the heat of the day, around noon, to draw water. Women from the village would usually travel to the well in the cool of the morning; furthermore, they walked together, not only for safety but also for community visiting along the way. The Samaritan woman was not accepted by the women of the community; thus she was an outcast. She would travel to the well alone when no one else was around.

I recall when the boys, and I attended a small Baptist Church in a rural town. I was the children's Sunday school teacher and the church pianist. One Sunday, the boys and I walked into church, and no one would make eye contact. Coy whispered to me that when he went to shake hands, they turned away. When the sermon was starting, I gathered the boys with my head hung down and headed to the door to leave. The pastor announced from the pulpit that "Satan has her family." We had fellowshipped there for several years. No one called to check on us; in fact, no one from that congregation even made eye contact or spoke to me again. At times I would encounter church members at the local grocery store; they would turn their head. I was at a loss to explain to the boys what had happened. Too often, churches attack the wounded. I was no longer welcomed in that place.

The Samaritan woman knew of God, was waiting for the Messiah, and knew what it meant to worship. In fact, she stated, "Our fathers worshiped on this mountain" (John 4:20), and "I know that Messiah is coming (who is called Christ). When He comes, He will tell us all things" (John 4:25). I wonder if her only hope was waiting for the Messiah to rescue her from her circumstances.

This Samaritan woman met Jesus at the well when she went to draw water. Jesus knew her past, "for you have had five husbands, and the one whom you now have is not your husband" (John 4:18). Many people in town knew her past and her current living situation. Obviously, those facts were not a secret, or the women in town would not have shunned her. However, this man (a Jew) was not from her town. I am sure she was puzzled, wondering how he could know those things about her. At that point, she responded, "Sir, I perceive that you are a prophet." I can feel her shame; I am sure she thought, "Great, even strangers know who I am and my past." I would have wanted to run and hide. Perhaps there was something different in his eyes, or the peace in his voice. In this story, her name is not recorded, only the Samaritan woman. I find that her name not recorded is out of compassion. Who would want their name recorded with those facts? I do not think John (the writer) even knew her name, only that Jesus (a Jew) was speaking with a Samaritan woman, which was against all cultural customs. She realized that she had met the Messiah when he responded, "I who speak to you am he" (John 4:26). Jesus offered her *living water,* forgiveness, and hope.

Olivia Lane sings a song, "Woman at the Well" (Lane Train Music 2021), which tells the story of "a brokenhearted woman who met the Savior of the world." In that song, the lyrics state, "I think that woman might be me." The words resonated with me. I certainly was the damaged, brokenhearted woman—two failed marriages, rejected, unloved, and unclean. I had made a choice to marry Dean when he was not a believer. I had made a choice to marry Leslie. I had been the first in my family to divorce and not once but twice. I needed the living water to fill me and wash over me. "My soul thirsts for God" (Psalm 42:2). "As the deer pants for the water so my soul longs after God" (Psalm 42:1). I related to the psalmist: "My tears have been my food day and night" (Psalm 42:3), "O my God, my soul is cast down within me" (Psalm 42:6).

Thank God for his compassion, that even in my destruction, he worked all things out for good for his purpose (Romans 8:28). I had repented and was clinging to the word of God. I would still make mistakes, but I would continue to run back to God. Just like the woman at the well, I was rescued by the Messiah.

Many people in that Samaritan City (Sychar) came to Christ because of her testimony (John 4:39–42). They would believe because of her testimony and because of their personal encounter with "Christ, the Savior of the world" (John 4:42). Would God be able to use my damaged past for his glory? Would my testimony of his faithfulness be able to bring people to Christ?

Sometime later, Leslie wrote me a letter. Leslie was a sponsor for guys in Alcoholic Anonymous (AA), and he firmly believed in working the "twelve steps." One of the steps was making amends. I knew he must be working through his own regrets.

My Dearest Kathleen,

What a foolish man I have been, especially to cause such harm to such a treasure as you. I have lied, told partial truths, lusted after others, and devastated your life. I began my relationship with you in hopes of finally getting it right, but I brought so much baggage to our home, including my own addictions, that I was not able to love you the way you should have been loved. I am a shallow, deceitful, and dishonest adulterer, who has caused you great pain. I can hardly bear the thought of the pain I caused you. I withdrew love and affection, often leaving you isolated and alone. I know that I am 100% responsible for your anxiety, strife, misery, and illness. I have caused all these disasters in your life, and if I could, I would repair the damage I have done. I can only humbly offer these amends and pray to our loving Father in heaven to heal your deep wounds. Sincerely, Leslie.

I would respond to Leslie's letter by simply mailing a card with the words "I forgive you" written inside. Occasionally, we would run into each other in our small town, but I avoided eye contact or conversation. I wanted to erase that chapter from my life and would love to delete this chapter from the book; however, to omit this chapter is to omit God's redeeming power and forgiveness in my life.

There are times when someone will hear my testimony and make remarks about my faithfulness or perseverance. I correct them every time. I was not faithful, God was faithful. I was not some spiritual tower; I was a broken woman. I made poor choices, *but God,* who is faithful, rescued me.

CHAPTER 5

The Struggle to Forgive

I had very little contact with Dean. I would take the kids to the prison twice a year if they wanted to go. I recall begging the guard to let me sit on the side of the visiting room when Dean and J.R. visited. The guard informed me that I had to sit at the table with them. I dreaded going to the prison, did not want to see Dean, and felt like it was torture for me. The boys were minors, so if they wanted to see their dad, an adult on the visitor's list had to accompany them into the prison. The trip was four hours each way. Besides the memories of how much Dean's decisions had hurt me through the years, the guards were often difficult; their language was horrible. One would make sexual comments to me. Others would treat me as if I was a felon too. We had to go through metal detectors, remove our shoes, and have our hands wiped and scanned. The guard would take a wand with a wet wipe attached to it and rub it all over our hands, then put it in a machine. If the machine buzzard went off, it meant that drug traces were detected, and then visits were denied or allowed only behind glass for thirty minutes. The car would be searched, and the visitor would be accused of having drugs or other illegal substances.

Twice that machine had gone off on me, once for heroin, and once for explosives. The sergeant came out. He accused me in a very firm voice, and the search began. If the visitor denied the search, then visits could be stopped permanently. If nothing was found in the search, the prison visitor was still behind glass with a nonworking phone; a guard sitting there, listening; and only thirty minutes in length. We would speak loudly and stand speaking in the metal grate mounted in the middle of the glass.

Trips to the prison involved not touching money for forty-eight hours prior (most money has traces of drugs), not touching doors or bathroom handles as we traveled, scrubbing with Clorox, wearing disposable gloves to avoid touching any drugs on surfaces, and lots of prayers. I hated that machine. If the machine went off three times in a year, visits could be denied permanently. I did research and found that although those machines were reliable (they would go off with even a trace of anything), they were not valid (just because I picked up something off money or a bathroom handle did not mean I had or did drugs). The sergeant would begin the incrimination, and the car would be thoroughly searched along with all belongings. They would dump everything out of luggage—the console, my purse— truly trashing everything. Often a drug dog would search with them. I would laugh at the craziness of it all if I could: schoolteacher mom brews meth and has explosives (too many television episodes of the show *Breaking Bad,* although I've never seen the show. Obviously, the guards must have watched the series). Anyone who visits a prison long enough is going to get dinged by the machine at one time or another. The stress of those visits was extreme. In the early years, I took a prescription antianxiety medication on days I would take the boys to the prison. After every visit, I would choke back the tears and vomit in the parking lot before heading home. Although the court never mandated that I take the kids to see Dean, J.R. wanted to see his dad. In the early years, Coy wanted to go too. I sacrificed my own feelings to take the boys once a year when possible.

Dean had written and asked me for the words of a song, "The Man," I had written years prior. I refused to send it to him. In that same letter he had written, he asked me to forgive him, proceeding by quoting Matthew 6:14–15: "If you do not forgive others [me], neither will your heavenly Father forgive you." The letter infuriated me. How dare Dean write and threaten me with God not forgiving me if I did not forgive him! In other words, he was implying, if I did not forgive him, I was going to hell. I was furious. He did not deserve my forgiveness. I did not hear Dean's heart, nor did I want to. The well of bitterness and unforgiveness rose in me. God continued to convict me. I needed to forgive Dean, not for Dean but for me. The bitterness and unforgiveness were poisoning me. Looking back in my prayer journals. I started working on forgiving Dean within a month of our separation. Years of journals were filled with entries working on forgiveness.

I once saw the movie *Amish Grace* (2010). The television film is based on a true story about the West Nickel Mines School shooting in Pennsylvania. A delivery man, a milkman, killed several Amish kids at a school. The Amish community demonstrated faith and forgiveness. There is a scene in the movie where a television news reporter inquires with a mother how she can possibly forgive the man that killed her daughters. The mother responds that she forgives moment by moment. She expands. saying, "Every time I think I hear one of them laughing in the house, I have to forgive again." Three of the Amish men went to see the wife of the man who committed the killings. When the wife asked why they would forgive such a horrible act, one Amish man stated, "We refuse to allow hatred in our hearts." I finally realized that forgiveness was not a feeling but a choice. I had to refuse to allow the bitterness and hatred to remain in my heart.

Matthew West released a song, "Forgiveness" (Anthem Entertainment 2012). I heard the song on the radio when driving home from work. The words pierced my heart: "It's the opposite of how you feel, when the pain they caused is just too real… Help me to do the impossible, forgiveness. It'll clear the bitterness away; it can even set a prisoner free… The prisoner that it really frees is you." I wanted to be free from the hurt and the bitterness I had carried so long. I knew the Bible stated that I must forgive "Even as Christ forgave you, so you also must do" (Colossians 3:13). In the book of Matthew, Peter asked Jesus how many times he should forgive a brother that sinned against him. Jesus answered, "I do not say to you up to seven times, but up to seventy times seven" (Matthew 18:21–22). I knew that God was calling me to forgiven Dean. The Bible was clear that I was to "let all bitterness and anger be put away from me… forgiving one another, just as Christ had forgiven" (Ephesians 4:31–32) me. Simply stated, forgiveness meant that I was to give up, to cease to feel angry (*Oxford American Dictionary*), and to let it go, giving up any desire to punish (*Webster's New World Dictionary*). I knew my bitterness was hindering my relationships with others and my relationship with God.

The next morning, when getting in the shower, I prayed, "Lord, give me the desire to want to forgive." I kept repeating that simple phrase. Weeks passed, and my prayers progressed to, "I choose to forgive in the name of Jesus. Lord, help me forgive." Choosing to forgive Dean was not about reconciliation; it was not about how I felt. It was only about freedom, my freedom from bondage.

One afternoon, I made a copy of the song Dean had requested, and only wrote three words, "I forgive you." I mailed the song, hoping I would not have to ever hear from Dean again. Our youngest, J.R., was going to be eighteen years old soon. I would no longer have to chaperone him into the prison to visit his dad. My life of prison visits was almost over. I could not imagine a day that I would forget all the hurt, but I could choose to forgive and no longer let that bitterness poison me.

The Song: The Man

1. I hit my knees in prayer
    Anger filled my soul
    How can I love this one
    So out of control
    He doesn't love you, Lord
    He doesn't care
    Can't you see his hatred
    And the bitterness he bears?
    Then a voice came to me
    So still and yet profound
    Tears fell down my face
    When I heard God's sound

Chorus

He said, "I...I died
For this one, I gave my life"
He said, "I...I died
For this one, I was crucified"

2.   *I couldn't just turn my head*
Tossing, turning in my bed,
I knew it was time to forgive
This man needed to see
The Lord's love through me,
It was time to receive God's peace
So if you see him on the street
If he's behind bars
No matter what he looks like
If you see his scars
The man you're looking at
He's loved by the King
Hold your judgment, friend
And remember this one thing

Chorus

A few days later, Dean called on the phone to speak to J.R. The phone was cutting in and out. J.R. was not home at that time. Dean had called on the house phone. J.R.'s cell phone had been broken, and we had yet to get it repaired. I picked up the house phone; it was a call from the prison. I simply stated, "J.R. is not home. Try back tomorrow night." Dean thanked me for sending the song. I asked, "Dean, why was I never enough?" At that time, the phone call abruptly ended. Days later, I received a letter in the mail from Dean.

5/21/12

Dear Kathleen,

I pray this letter finds you well. I'm writing not knowing when or even if I will be able to talk to you again, and there are things I must tell you. After our last conversation Friday night, right when the phone was cutting off, your crackling voice hung in the air as you asked the question, "Why was I not enough?" My heart was breaking. I wanted to comfort you, but we were out of time. There was no chance of calling back that night. I called the next morning, hoping to talk; however, I was unable to do so.

God has filled the hole that I used to try and fill with sex and drugs. I now really believe. I try not to just read the Bible; I try to live the way the Bible tells me to live. To answer your question, "Why am I not enough?" Kath, it is not you. I want you to know that you're a good woman, the best I've even known. I also want you to know that you had nothing to do with my cheating. Oh, sure, I had all the excuses. Tears are filling my eyes as I tell you, I traded the truth of God for a lie. I'm the horrible person Paul speaks of in Romans, chapter 1. If I could just go back and know what I know now, I would show you what a good husband Jesus has made me; however, I realize that can't be.

It's crazy, but just a little while ago, I put on my headphones, and the song "Healing Rain" came on. I pray for that healing rain to wash over you Kath. God bless and keep you.

Dean

I had waited years to hear that apology. Years for Dean to take responsibility for his actions. I thought hearing those words would somehow miraculously heal all the rejections and hurt. Dean continued to write, but I was not in a place to receive his letters. I would open them, only to scan them briefly and throw them in a cloth box stored at the top of the closet. I never intended to read through the pile of letters carefully, much less believe his claims of conversation to Christianity.

In my experience, forgiveness has never been a one-time event. In 2 Corinthians 10:5, Paul stated, "We take captive every thought to make it obedient to Christ." When those memories triggered unforgiveness, I had to take captive those thoughts and once again yield them to God and pray to forgive. I reflected on my life with Dean and my life with Leslie. With both, addiction had destroyed them, though the addictions were different. Leslie too had struggled with alcoholism at one time, although he had twenty years of alcohol sobriety when I had met him. I compared their actions to what God defines as love in 1 Corinthians 13. I sat down and wrote "The Marriage Vows of an Addict."

The Marriage Vows of the Addict
I Cor. 13:4–7 (NIV and The Message)

I promise to be self-centered
Love cares more for others than self

I promise to envy, lust, and desire others
Love doesn't want what it doesn't have

I promise to put my feelings first
Love isn't always me first

I promise to lie, keep secrets, and tell partial truths
Love takes pleasure in flowering of the truth

I promise to yell, curse, and explode
Love doesn't fly off the handle

I promise to hurt you emotionally and perhaps physically
Love always protects and looks for the best

I promise to be manipulative
Love is not self-seeking

I promise to neglect you and withhold love
Love is kind

In my addiction, I'm incapable of love
Love never gives up

CHAPTER 6

The Prisoner's Mite

Once again, I opened the mailbox to find an envelope from the *correctional facility*. This time, inside was a check. On the memo line, it stated, "family support." The check was written for $20. *Odd*, I thought. We had never received a check from the facility before, and certainly I found $20, ironic as *family support*, perhaps, a fast-food hamburger for the boys but certainly not family support. The checks kept coming. One morning, J.R. was in the kitchen. He mentioned that Dad was sending money for our Africa mission trip. J.R. was a senior in high school, and we were going to go on a mission trip to Zambia after he graduated high school in May. Each month, I would cash the checks and put the money in our jar in the kitchen. We had a large jar in the kitchen cabinet, decorated with photos of Africa. We were saving to be able to go on a mission trip.

I had not discussed the money with Dean. If J.R. had not told me, I would not have known it was for the mission trip and that the money out of Dean's salary. I was aware that prisoners held jobs in prison, and that income paid for them to put money on their account to make phone calls and purchase commissary items. Dean had held various jobs in prison: pod porter (cleaning the prison pod), blood-borne-pathogen clean-up guy, woodshop tutor. Most of his time, Dean was working for the education division as a GED math tutor.

One day, J.R. mentioned that Dad made sixty cents an hour in prison. Previously, Dean made thirty cents an hour. I heard the comment but did not really give it much attention. The months passed, and the checks kept coming. One day, I heard, "Kath, sixty cents an hour." I knew it was that still, small voice of God. I sat down with a calculator, the checks equaled 90 percent of everything Dean made. I had heard that Dean had given his life to Christ in prison. He had written to tell me, and others had mentioned it to me. I was skeptical about prison religion. Several research studies indicated the benefits of religion in prison diminish and become insufficient over time once the inmate is discharged. One longitudinal study by Penn State and Florida State University, looking at a Pennsylvania prison, found that involvement in religious activities while incarcerated did not decrease recidivism (a return to prison later). Other studies indicated that very few continue to attend religious activities once they are discharged from prison. I did not doubt that Dean was attending church in prison; what I doubted was that Dean had truly had an encounter with Jesus and that he was a changed man.

I knew that prison food was undesirable; they rarely were given beef. Most meals were ground turkey meat, plant and soy-based meat, or chicken. Prisoners often used their income to buy food from the commissary, such as soup, crackers, or even coffee. In addition, they had to purchase their own toothpaste, T-shirts, tennis shoes, socks, underwear, or additional toilet paper. I also knew that commissary was very expensive, over 110 percent markup compared to groceries on the outside. Dean had been sending his entire check, minus 10 percent for months; I knew 10 percent was the tithing amount. My eyes filled with tears.

Jesus told a story in the Bible of the widow's mite. In Mark 12:41–44, it states, "Now Jesus sat opposite of the treasury and saw how the people put money into the treasury. And many who were rich put in much. Then one poor widow came and threw in two mites, which makes a quadrans." A mite was the smallest coin in Palestine and worth about one-eighth of a cent. "So He called His disciples to Himself and said to them, 'Assuredly, I say to you that this poor widow has put in more than all those who have given to the treasury; for they all put in out of their abundance, but she out of her poverty put in all that she had, her whole livelihood.'" Could it truly be possible that Dean was sending us all he had out of his poverty, a prisoner's mite?

I had been sarcastic about the small amount of money in the checks; but it was ***all*** he had. In our divorce, Dean did not give us any money except that stated in the divorce settlement for monthly child support. Even that amount stopped after he was incarcerated. Dean had a significant 401(k), but that money was all used in his legal defense. The kids and I had not received any of that money. In that moment, God began to soften my heart. Why would Dean give us all he had? The journey of healing had begun.

CHAPTER 7

Africa

J.R. graduated from high school, and we headed to Zambia Africa. We had never traveled internationally. The multiple plane connections, immigration checks, luggage checks proved to be quite stressful. Five other youth had joined us for the trip; we met up with them at other airports during our travel. They would all fall asleep in airports as we waited for our next connection. I was far too fearful to sleep and kept watch over the sleeping youth and their travel bags. After three days of travel, exhausted, and legs swollen from days sitting on planes, desperately needing a shower, we arrived in Johannesburg, Africa. From there, we caught a small plane to Zambia. Once at the mission base in Zambia, we would shower, sleep in a tent for the night, and eat a warm meal. Later we would head out to the villages in the bushland of Zambia. We would pile into a large military vehicle and travel for another twelve hours to arrive at our destination.

"Ma-wuka buti?" is a morning greeting, meaning "How did you wake up?" The sunrise was incredible. Each team member crawled out of their tents to gather around for morning breakfast and the morning devotional. There was no running water (except at scattered and scarce boreholes, which could be a day's travel), no electricity, and no bathrooms (except a circular structure made from straw and inside a hole in the dirt). The structure, a rough similarity to an outhouse, was called a "long drop." With enough imagination, one

can determine why it was called a long drop. Obviously, aim was important.

I had dreamed of going into the bushland of Africa since college, when I had a college friend who served there in the mission field. Finally, I was walking on the soil, listening to the sounds of the natives' chant around the fire at dark and able to share the love of Jesus. God had laid Africa on my heart for years. I thought the call on my life was to serve in Africa full-time. In fact, after I returned to the United States, I thought I would return soon to the villages. God did call me to Africa in that season but not for the purposes I had imagined.

Alcoholism was prevalent in this culture. They made it from fermented corn. I related to the women in the villages because I understood what it was like to live with alcoholism; Dean had been a drinker. We would walk to various huts and minister to the villagers there. A translator would travel with us. I recall once when a male translator would not translate my message, I was speaking to an abused woman and telling her about my husband and the power of God. The translator later asked me why I would make up such a story about my husband being in prison or his alcoholism. He did not believe that I was telling the truth; after all, I was from America, and he believed everything was perfect in America.

My precious tentmate, Mama Lenah, was a native woman who had the HIV virus, had lost her husband to murder, and had a son in prison. We traveled and preached together for two weeks. She was such a precious sister in Christ, and I knew God had "bunked" us together. My heart burned with passion for Zambia. Even as I write now, I still feel the love for the people there. Mama Lenah gave me a native name: Milimo. She said it meant "one of joy."

As we walked into a village one day, Rosa came out of the hut. She immediately took my hand and led me to her hut. She had mistaken me for another missionary that had come years before. She came out of the hut with Cecilia by her side. I guessed Cecilia was between twelve to fifteen years old. A white picnic chair served as a seat to a metal frame with wheels, a rough version of a wheelchair.

Cecilia had no control over responses, including eye contact, and no verbal communication. It was clear that she had been born with a disability, probably cerebral palsy by the manifestation of symptoms. Her breathing was laborious, and her mother, Rosa, walked bent over from back problems, lifting Cecilia for years. Rosa looked aged from her years as a caregiver of a child with cerebral palsy. She complained of back, hip, and leg pain.

Cecilia made utterances. Rosa stated that Cecilia never talked. But after the missionaries came three years ago, the utterance started. They sounded much like someone praying in tongues. As I spoke with Cecilia, her eyes registered understanding. Somehow, I knew this child knew Jesus and understood far more than we knew.

So often when in Africa, I felt as if we were standing on holy ground. I never felt so much joy as I did when I was laughing with the children in the village or dancing around the campfire in worship with the locals. I spent time with Chief Simwatchela. He let me go into a fifth-grade class to visit with the children. He said he would be praying for my return. One of the guides, Bornwell, asked me not to forget Africa or the people. I promised I would not.

Joy had certainly been lacking in my life, but that name given to me planted a seed. I would later search the scripture for joy, and it would become my favorite word. Even today, my home has the word *joy* displayed in numerous places.

One hot afternoon, the Americans had a soccer match against some of the villagers. Quite a crowd had gathered around, traveling in from the villages. The American missionaries were no match for these men and boys. The locals played barefoot and seem to fly in the air. After the match, my son J.R. was chosen to preach. He stood up with my tentmate translating for him. He talked about being raised without a dad in the home. He talked about his dad in prison. The honesty and vulnerability in that moment was so significant because J.R. had not told anyone about his dad being in prison to my knowledge. His dad had already been incarcerated for seven years. J.R. would tell people his dad was in this town or that town, wherever Dean had been transferred, but implied he worked there. J.R. preached about how difficult it had been: his dad, his stepdad

(Leslie), the rejection, the abandonment, and alcoholism. I stood in the back, sobbing. I could not control the tears and the shame I felt. At the same time, I was so proud of J.R.; he was powerfully speaking to the crowd. He talked about how God was his dad. I can still hear his sermon in my head after all these years. When he asked the crowd, who wanted God to be their dad, dozens of men and boys stood up everywhere, receiving Christ.

I immediately recognized the faithfulness of God, recalling my prayer for so many years: "Lord, you promised in your word you are a father to the fatherless. Raise my boys" (Psalm 68:5). God had heard my prayer! The boys never knew my prayer, but there was J.R., standing in front of a crowd and referring to God as his dad. I was overwhelmed with the faithfulness of God. I cried for hours; the tears would not stop. God had heard my prayers all those years. He had raised J.R. up to be a mighty warrior for God. In Africa, God told me I would have to give him J.R. I fought in prayer but finally surrendered J.R.

The Bible (1 Samuel) tells a story of a woman named Hannah. She was married to a man named Elkanah, who loved her. Hannah longed to have a child; however, the "Lord had closed her womb" (1 Samuel 1:6). Year after year, Hannah would travel with Elkanah to the city to worship and make sacrifices to the Lord. She went to the tabernacle and "prayed to the Lord and wept in anguish" (1 Samuel 1:10). She refused to eat. Elkanah tried to comfort his wife, asking her if he was not enough: "Am I not better to you than ten sons" (1 Samuel 1:8)? Hannah continued to pray in the tabernacle, "O Lord of hosts… remember me, do not forget me. Give me a male child, then I will give him to [you] all the days of his life" (1 Samuel 1:11).

Eli was the priest at the tabernacle. He had watched Hannah. Although her lips were moving, she was not speaking any words aloud. Eli assumed Hannah was drunk and scolded her, "How long will you be drunk? Put your wine away" (1 Samuel 1:14)! Honestly, this priest did not have a clue! Hannah was overwhelmed with sadness and crying out to God. Did Eli not see the tears streaming down her face? Had Eli never been around a grieving woman? She told Eli that she was not intoxicated but rather "poured out [her] soul before the Lord" (1 Samuel 1:15). At this comment, Eli answered, "Go in peace and may the God of Israel grant your petition" (1 Samuel 1:18). I am impressed by Hannah's composure with Eli. She was at church, crying out to God, and the priest accused her of being drunk.

Hannah did become pregnant, and she named her son Samuel. She rejoiced at God's faithfulness, and her prayer of thanksgiving is recorded in 1 Samuel 2. In that prayer, she stated, "My heart rejoices in the Lord" (1 Samuel 2:1). Hannah kept her promise to God. When Samuel was weaned, she took him to the tabernacle to serve (and learn) under Eli the priest. Hannah gave Samuel to the Lord. "I have lent him to the Lord; as long as he lives, he shall be lent to the Lord" (1 Samuel 1:28). I must admit that I am astonished that she took him to Eli, the same priest that accused her of being drunk. There is no indication that Hannah felt any bitterness over the misunderstanding in the tabernacle that day. Samuel "grew and the Lord was with him" (1 Samuel 3:19). Samuel became a prophet and a leader in all of Israel. He was a mighty man for the kingdom of God. The Lord blessed Hannah with more children, six in total. She had three more sons and two daughters.

Just as Hannah went to the temple and gave Samuel to the work of the Lord (1 Samuel), God was pressing me to release J.R. to his work. The last night in Africa, we sat around a firepit and shared what God was speaking to each of us. I knew, in that moment, that God was telling me to give him J.R. The story of Hannah played in my mind. I wanted the word from the Lord to be telling me that I would return, but instead, God was pressing on me to surrender my son. J.R. would return to Africa and later to other countries. He would surrender to the ministry after that trip and serve full-time in the mission field. In 2012, J.R. would get married in Israel to his precious wife, Rose. J.R. got married while in the mission field. I never imagined that I would not attend my own son's wedding, but it happened. I looked through the photos of his wedding. I had never seen such joy on his face. I knew, in that moment, he and his young bride would make a difference for the kingdom of God. To this date, J.R. and his wife, with their three children, serve in full-time ministry, reaching the nations for God.

I returned to the United States. I enrolled in a Bible school and began to take coursework. I had decided that I was going to leave my position at the university as an associate professor within the next two years, and I was going to pursue the ministry. I needed to prepare for this transition and become equipped. I was back in America, but my heart had stayed in Africa.

In my prayer time, God convicted me, "Kath, how could you go to Africa and preach to the *nations* that, in Christ, the old is passed away, and they are a new creation (2 Corinthians 5:17) but not believe it in your own family?" I knew God was referring to Dean. Dean and I had been divorced for eight years now. Dean had written several times through the years, telling me that he had accepted Christ, asking for forgiveness; and shared what God had done in his life. I never responded to those comments by Dean, nor did I believe that he had changed. My faith was shaken, that core belief is the very foundation of Christianity, that in Christ, we are new creation. Did I believe in the power of Christ to transform lives or not? Early in Dean's incarceration, I had written to him and quoted that exact verse in 2 Corinthians. I had told him he could become a new creation. However, I came to realize that in my heart, I never truly *believed* it could happen, especially for Dean.

CHAPTER 8

The Letters

I got out the stepladder and climbed up, reaching the cloth box at the top of the closet. I poured out the pile of letters from Dean onto the floor. The letters surrounded me. My heart was pounding, tears flowing down my face. I read one letter at a time. Hours passed; I remained captivated reading the letters.

7/8/12

Dear Kathleen,

  Like Paul started His letter to the saints at Philippi, "Grace to you, and peace from God our Father and the Lord Jesus Christ. I thank God upon every remembrance of you always in my prayers, making request for you with joy." I don't know, Kath, if you can tell from my letters that I've changed. I don't know if you can tell that I'm not the man I used to be, and I guess I should not care what you think of me. I do care, and there is no denying it; there's a place over my heart that you guard. Oh, I've tried to fill that place with other things booze & bimbos. As you can tell, that didn't work out so well. I believe that place will always be yours, regardless

57

of the other people we have in our lives. When I said until death do us part, I didn't know what I was saying, but God did (Mark 11:23). I was devastated when you married Leslie. I wanted to beg and plea with you, "No, Kath, don't." What I failed to realize, those feelings were God-given. I will not make that mistake again. Kathleen, I love you till death, and you are the one that guards my heart. And if we cannot be reconciled, I pray death comes soon because life sucks without you. PS. My friend Demas said at least send a card saying RIP.

Dean

12/16/2012

Dear Kathleen,

There's something I would like to apologize for, first for apparently demanding forgiveness from you. I will not deny that either, but you have me at somewhat of a disadvantage since you have my letters to refer too; all I have is my failing memory. So taking all that into consideration, I'm going to say I'm sorry for contributing to the delay in your process of forgiveness. I believe sometimes I want to show you so badly how diligent I am about studying the word of God that perhaps I am a little overzealous. I'm searching for the truth, like you. I want what God wants for us. The last thing I want is to upset you. Kath, what is to happen in the future, I do not know. Whatever does happen, I want to thank you for my children, for 16 years of faithful love, but most of all for planting the seed in which it was watered and led to my salvation. If there is in fact two questions when we get to heaven, you can tell them you brought me.

God bless and keep you. With love,
Dean

12/17/2012

Dear Kathleen,

I just mailed a letter to you this morning. You are absolutely, positively the most beautiful woman I've ever seen. You're glowing. I believe it is the glory of God shining in you. I showed some photos to some of my friends and told them you are more beautiful today than the day I married you.

You know, Kath, I really thought that God had told me to write you conveying my feelings about my beliefs, about my heart, and soul. It's been several months. The correction officer passed out the mail. I gathered around again, and once again, no response from you. I came back to my cell and sat on my bed. I once again started going over my thoughts on divorce, wondering if God wanted me to be single for the rest of my life. I want God's will for me. I feel like Jonah, and I'm tired of being in the belly of the fish.

You may think being an Elder, an associate pastor, or a pastor in a prison church is not a real church. I believe we are under even more scrutiny. Where others get to go home, go on vacation, or away from their congregation, we are never away from our congregation. When we eat, go to recreation, go to sleep, go to shower, for crying out loud, even in the bathroom, we are under the microscope 24-7 and 365 days a year. And if that is not enough, we are always on camera. I'm saying all this to tell you that God finally got ahold of me. You know I never do things halfway; if I was drinking, I was getting drunk. That is how I serve God, all or nothing.

I often think about the stupid mistakes I've made; there's so many. One that sticks worse than any other, probably because I wasn't drinking, do you remember when Coy got that one haircut that all the other boys had, it kind of looked like a bowl? You and Coy came out to where I was welding. He was so happy. I can't remember the words I spoke, but I do know they were hurtful and cruel. You turned around and took Coy back to town to have them recut his hair. I was responsible for breaking that little boy's heart, God's gift to me. There was nothing to blame, no alcohol, no working late, nothing...just my sinful nature. I feared what people were going to say. What would my grandmother say about his haircut? Honestly, Kath, I don't know why you stayed with me as long as you did. I've told Coy how sorry I am. He says he doesn't even remember it, but I do. I sure wish I could just go back, snatch that little boy up, and hug him so tight and tell him how much I love him. I don't know if any of those wounds will ever heal.

Please hug the boys for me. God bless you.

Dean

12/28/2012

Dear Kath,

Kath, can I please have your cell phone number? There's a couple of reasons for this. The first being, like I said before, I love you, and I'm not going to say I think; I know. Second, I would want to talk to you even if you did not look like you, even if you were 85 years old. I know you are hot, and I want to talk to the hottest woman I know. Third, I know you are spending time with another man you want to get to know. I know life is not fair, but this is so unfair. You already have a bad taste in your mouth because you knew me when I was the other guy, not the God-fearing man I am today. To make this somewhat fair, we either need to not let the other guys talk to you or even email or see you face-to-face or to let me at least have a chance to phone you.

Love,
Dean

1/1/13

Kathleen,

Happy New Year! Hey, I woke up without a headache and without a hangover for the 6th year in a row on New Year's Day, and I feel good.

I was listening to the radio this morning, and a song came on; it was about an 80-year-old man that still remembered the first fight he had with his wife and how he should have just gone home and gave her a hug. That pride is such an awful thing; it's what got Satan kicked out of heaven. It's what got me kicked out of the house. I should of gave you a hug and said, "I'm sorry." I wonder if I'll ever say I'm sorry enough, probably not; however, I have learned something through all this, being sorry is not enough; it takes change. I can't believe it took losing you, the kids, prison for me to realize that I was heading for hell and, what's worse, probably leading my children there also. I'm sorry, Kath, I wasn't the godly man you

deserved. I'm sorry I wasn't the godly dad the boys deserved. In James, it tells us (James 1:14), "But each one is tempted when he is drawn away by his own desires and enticed. Then when desire has conceived it gives birth to sin; and sin, when it is full-grown brings forth death." I was blinded by that sin. I've got a God that breaks the chains of addictions. He sets the prisoners free. I thank Him that He sets me free.
    God Bless and keep you.

Love,
Dean

9/16/2013

Dear Kathleen,

    I have spent the last 6 months, wondering what I wrote to upset you so much to warrant the nonreply to my letters; it was really bothering me to say the least. I tried and tried to remember what I said. Was it because I told you I love you? You have no idea how much I hate the man I used to be. I dishonored God, and I claimed to be a Christian. Kath, I don't want to "pick up where we left off." That man is dead, with no hope of resurrection. Tears well up in my eyes as I try to convey who I am, what I do, what I want. What I want is just a chance to show you what God has done with me. No commitment, just communication, whether by letter or phone, is all up to you. I would love to bike and walk with you. Does that scare you? You know the old guy would have never said that (haha).

God bless and keep you,
Dean

10/30/2013

Hey, Kathleen,

I know it is not your birthday; however, this is the only card I could find. I wanted to thank you for the newspaper clippings of J.R. I would be lying if I said I wasn't disappointed I haven't received a letter from you. It reminds me of being a little puppy when they call, "Mail," tongue hanging out, wagging my tail, and then nothing. My head hangs down, tail between my legs, and I walk back to my cell. I pray everything is all right with you all. God bless and keep you.

Dean

Nov. 11, 2013

Dear Kathleen,

The morning of the 22nd, I was deep in prayer. I told God, "It does not matter whether I'm alone the rest of my life; all that matters is you, Lord." That day, your letter (the song) showed up. Do you believe in coincidence? I do not.

I've heard some sermons in here lately that are really bothering me. They were name it, claim it, blab it, grab it, trying always to make you feel good. You know the type. It doesn't matter what you do; God loves you, the same kind of sermons that put this country boy in the state of corrections department. Then Ezek. 33:8 came to my mind: "I have made you a watchman. Therefore, you shall hear a word from *my mouth and speak to warn them for me." Needless to say, I'm a preacher.*

Dean

I read one letter after another, all sharing portions of his biblical studies and what he was learning, testimonies of other inmates coming to Christ, portions of sermons he had written and preached, and pleas to open the lines of communication with him, often mentioning his mistakes and how he was no longer that man. There I sat, in the middle of the floor, with letters dumped on the floor. Years of letters that Dean had sent from prison to me. I never read them to hear Dean's heart. Several years of letters were all scattered, letters about how he had found Christ, letters about how he learned what it means to love from the Holy Spirit, letters about wanting his family, letters about God's grace. He wrote other specifics to substantiate his claims: "Take the cowboys for instance. I would prefer they still win, but I would rather be in the church than watching the game, hmm... go figure." He wrote how he loved me, and *he knew*. Early in our dating relationship, he told me he loved me and then followed it by saying, "I think." I read one letter after another, tears running down my face. Hours passed as I sat and read through each handwritten letter. I began to pray, "Lord, if you want me to return to my marriage, you are going to have to give me love for my husband." Slowly, my heart began to change, not a change that occurs overnight. My heart had harbored bitterness for years. Unfortunately, it took years for me to fall deeply back in love with my husband. Night fell, and I continued to read. I fell asleep in the early morning hours on the floor, surrounded by tear-stained letters.

In the morning, I dialed the number of the prison. "Hello, could you please tell me who the chaplain is?" My stomach was in knots as I made that call to the prison facility. The voice on the phone responded.

"Is there a way I can reach him?" I asked. "Yes, please, I would appreciate him calling me." I proceeded to give my name and number. Later that day, Chaplain Montoya called. He inquired how he could assist me. I explained that I was the ex-wife of an inmate. I asked him if he knew Dean. I told him that Dean had claimed he had accepted Christ. I concluded that if Dean was really walking the walk, perhaps the prison chaplain would know him and could either validate or discredit Dean's story of conversion. I briefly said that Dean was not a very good person when we were married. Chaplain listened quietly. Then he spoke gently, "Mrs. Tayler, I don't know anything about your ex-husband. I only know Dean. He is a man that is dedicated to Christ. He has been the pastor here for five years. He is a good man." I thanked the chaplain and hung up the phone. Could it be possible that 2 Corinthians 5:17 is true; when a man (woman) comes to Christ, the old is passed away, and they are a new creation?

I read the book of Hosea. Gomer was a prostitute (a harlot). She was desired, lusted after, and wanted by men. They would give her fine clothes and jewelry of silver and gold. She had all the material possessions she wanted. She was not the type of girl a man would marry; she had accepted that fate. I am sure she must have been puzzled when Hosea pursued her, not in a way she had become accustomed to but with unconditional love. He would marry her. Even after marriage, she would run back to her life of prostitution. He would go back after her and bring her home again.

Not many pastors share the story of Hosea and Gomer from the pulpit for obviously reasons. A church full of innocent children and the story of prostitution probably would not be a popular choice. However, I heard the story three times in that one year. I cannot recall ever hearing anyone preach on the book of Hosea prior to that year, and I have not heard it since—truly the greatest love story ever told, a story of a man that pursues a woman with godly intentions, unconditional love, and forgiveness in his heart. Furthermore, the book of Hosea is a story of how God continues to forgive and pursue his people.

I've never liked the name Gomer for this woman. I grew up in the days of *Andy Griffith*, and the name Gomer reminds me of Gomer Pyle (a character in the TV show). Hosea sounds like Hannah or something similar, a girl's name. Regardless of their names, God was showing me he wanted me to chase after and forgive Dean (my ex-husband). Dean was not a prostitute; however, there had been plenty of infidelity in the marriage. Although the Bible allows for divorce in such circumstances, I felt God was calling me back to my marriage. I admitted to God that I did not have the desire to forgive Dean, nor did I have the strength.

Just as Gomer ran back to her old life, and Hosea went after her, I felt like God was telling me to go after Gomer (Dean). He was so unworthy of forgiveness from me; after all, consider all he had done. I did not think I could ever forget the past, much less forgive those events. I was right; I could not. Only through God would I be able to forgive. I would surrender those memories; they were God's, and I could no longer hold on to the hurt.

In my pride, I could list everything Dean had done wrong. Only through spiritual maturity would I come to realize that I too am Gomer. God had forgiven me again and again, he pursued me, he forgave me, and he continues to chase after me. I am unworthy of God's forgiveness, but he gave it anyway. I too run back to things; God pursues me. I thought I would be doing Dean a great favor to forgive him. Time would show me that the one who would receive the greatest blessings would be me.

CHAPTER 9

A Lonely Thanksgiving

I woke early and began the cooking and preparation for Thanksgiving. The next day was Thanksgiving. My favorite holiday has always been Thanksgiving. I decorated for the holiday with all my fall decor early in October. My favorite colors are yellow and orange. All three boys were living with me, and tomorrow was my favorite day of the year.

Coy had recently graduated from the police academy. He was moving out (again). He had moved back home during his time at the academy, coming home on weekends. He had told me that he had rented a place in town. He was up early, packing his things. Apparently, some friends were coming over with a flatbed trailer to help him move. I hated that he was moving out. I enjoyed having him home but certainly understood. He was working as a patrol officer and had a steady job.

I was in the kitchen baking pies when his friends arrived and backed the trailer into the drive. I glanced out the front window. The morning was crisp with a chill in the air. By this time, both J.R. and C.J. were up too. I thought the boys were up to help Coy load his belongings. I turned to see J.R. and C.J. loading J.R.'s bed and dresser onto the flatbed trailer. J.R. and C.J. were moving out with Coy. All the boys were grown. J.R. and C.J. had part-time jobs and were in college at the local university. However, at no time had the boys mentioned to me that they were *all* moving out. Coy snapped at his brothers, "I told you guys that you were going to have to tell Mom!"

I questioned Coy, "How could you not tell me?"

Coy responded that he had told J.R. he had to tell me. The boys continued to load the trailer and proceeded to pack up their rooms.

There had been no argument, no huge fight, and no warning. The boys just felt it was time to be on their own. I knew eventually my boys would grow up and move out but all at once, without discussion, and the day before Thanksgiving!

The phone rang, and J.R. handed me his phone, "Mom, it's Dad. He wants to talk to you." I reluctantly took the phone and walked out to the garage. Apparently, J.R. had told his dad they were all moving out.

"Hello," I said.

Dean asked, "Kath, are you okay?"

"Of course, I'm not okay! You knew?" I asked.

Dean continued to talk calmly, "That's why I called."

I cannot recall much more of the conversation, only that he was compassionate and tried to soothe me. Prison calls are only twenty minutes long, and he had been on the phone with J.R. prior to handing the phone to me. The conversation was brief.

The house felt empty that night. I walked by the empty bedrooms. I heard the heater come on, and it rattled. I never knew the heater had a rattling noise before. I remember lying in bed, listening to the clock as it ticked; that clock was so loud. I got up and removed the batteries. I had never heard that clock before. My home had been full of activity with the three boys and their friends, never quiet.

On Thanksgiving Day, Coy had to work. C.J. went to spend the day with his grandmother. J.R. stopped by for a short time midafternoon but had already eaten. I put all the food in the freezer bags. I cut up the turkey and the ham and put portions in freezer bags. I gave away the pies. I called Coy to come take some of the food down to the police station for those working; he commented they had a potluck and already had plenty. I had a huge meal prepared, and no one was at home. I did not even eat the Thanksgiving meal.

I took the dog and went for a walk around the university campus. There were many others out, walking after their Thanksgiving lunch. The day had warmed up, and the fresh air did me good. My life had revolved around the boys for as long as I could remember. I hated that they moved out. I remember when the boys first stopped playing sports their senior years, I had no friends and did not know what to do with my time. Every night I had sat at practices or games with other sports moms. Suddenly, my entire network of friends was gone, and just like that, our commonalty had ended. Coming home and fixing dinner for the boys and sometimes their friends are gone. I now would make dinner for one, which most of the time ended up being a bowl of cereal. Many of my working peers had families or at least a spouse at home. There were few people in my life that were available to go get dinner, go to a movie, or hang out.

I would call an old friend, Jack, that lived 250 miles away to come up and be my date for university events that invited me and a guest. Jack was sweet and always my standby, although there was no romantic relationship. We had been friends for over twenty years. His daughter was the same age as my boys, and years ago we had lived in the same town and served in the children's ministry together. His life had taken many sad turns through the years, and he lost his way, but we remained steady, reliable friends. My life felt empty and lonely. Once again, I was at a place where I desperately needed Jesus. Day to day it was just Jesus and me. I felt like everyone else in my life left me.

CHAPTER 10

Reconciliation

Dean continued to write. I wrote to Dean, giving him permission to call me. Dean would call a couple of times a week. By the middle of December, I agreed to travel to the prison to visit him. The trip was approximately two hundred miles one way. I would have to get up early to be in line to enter the prison at 8:00 a.m. Only a certain number of visitors are allowed each day. I entered the prison's waiting room. The room was cold, with white walls of brick, with a guard sitting nearby. I was to sit on one side of the table, and Dean would come in and sit on the other side. "Don't touch, not feet, not hands, and stay on your side of the table," the guard told me. I felt like I was going to vomit; I had always been one to vomit when I was upset or anxious.

Dean entered the room, smiled at me, and walked over. I was incredibly uncomfortable. The words did not come easy. I was sure I was going to hear every excuse: "I was framed." "I am innocent." "It was not my fault." "What really happened was…" I had braced myself. I saw Dean wipe his eye with his hand. "Was he crying?" surely not. I had been with Dean for sixteen years and never saw him cry, even though at times I saw his eyes water, a tear had never fallen. I recalled once in our marriage during the middle of the night. I rolled over in bed and realized Dean was awake. I asked him if he was all right and touched his face in the dark; it was wet. We had just found out his mom had cancer. I thought he must be crying that night, but he denied it.

He sat down at the table. He said, "Kath, I'm so sorry. It is all my fault. You were a wonderful wife and a great mother." I looked into his eyes; they were soft and gentle. I noticed how still he sat. Dean never sat still; his right leg always shook when he was sitting. I never recalled him taking responsibility for any actions. There were always excuses and lies. There was a different peace about him, and he sat still. His first sentence took total responsibility and no excuses. His eyes and body posture were peaceful.

Another inmate entered the room, proceeding to another table to sit with a visitor. He stopped as he passed and shook Dean's hand. "Pastor," he said. Did he just call my wild ex-husband pastor? The prison allowed me to stay five hours that day. We talked through the years of hurt. Dean admitted to everything: the adultery, the mistakes, the way he had treated me, his drinking, and his responsibility in the accident that ended him in prison. There were no excuses, only deep apologies, often wiping the tears from his eyes. Dean told me he forgave me for writing the statement to the judge, even though that letter (statement) had hurt him deeply. He chose to let go of that resentment. He told me he understood why I married Leslie, and Dean felt responsible for my choices.

I was emotionally exhausted and cried most of the four-hour drive home. Where do I go from here, Lord? The scriptures say that "God give light to those in darkness, a way of peace" (Luke 1:79). Dean had the light of Jesus and was filled with peace.

The guard announced, "Five minutes." People stood up to hug their loved one goodbye and give a quick kiss goodbye. Dean stood and hugged me and then quickly kissed me on the mouth! I was shocked and caught off guard. I then followed the line of visitors out the door and to the parking lot. I vomited in the dirt on the side of the parking lot and then proceeded to my vehicle and drove home. I remember crying and praying all the way home. So many emotions flooded me; it was all truly overwhelming. There were too many feelings to process, and I was exhausted mentally and emotionally.

Dec. 13, 2013

Dean,

There is so much more I want to say to you, ask about, and try to understand. I'm not the same woman I was ten years ago. You claim you are not the same man... That is obvious, but I'm not the same woman. So what if the woman I am today is not the woman you still love?

A long time ago, we had a son, Coy, that was following peer pressure. He was being very rebellious. We packed up the family and got away. We stayed in a tent. During that time, Coy calmed down. He was restored. We were restored, away...in a tent. This last summer, I once again found myself in a tent, a tent with little else but a God-fearing roommate that was 42, a sister in Christ, Mama Lenah, and HIV positive... There, in a tent, I found life again.

In addition...since we need to get to know each other...here are some things about me (and yes that means each letter you must tell me things about you because I really don't know you now).

1. I like yellow. It's cheerful. I've painted one bathroom yellow ever since you left.
2. My favorite color is orange. You gave me an orange guitar once. It's still my favorite guitar and the only guitar I still own. I haven't played the guitar in years.
3. I've prayed in tongues, rarely with others...but in Africa tons.
4. Jer. 29:11 is my life verse. God gave me that verse years ago... It has held me in dark hours. It reminds me that God has hope and future for me.

5.   A couple of years ago, I refurbished an old secretary... It's one of my favorite pieces of furniture. My dad bought the glass for me. I purposely left some "scars" on it... "It reminds me of God's faithfulness" and my own scars.

What are your hopes? What are your dreams? What do you want? What makes you laugh? What makes you happy? What makes you sad?

Kath

12/17/2013

Dear Kath,

I don't believe it; I received a letter from a very sweet gal today. What are my dreams? To make a difference in people's lives, not just to be a pew—warming Christian! My wants? You are by my side (no pressure, you asked). What makes me laugh? To tell you the truth, the last nine years have not led to many laughs; however, the last couple of weeks have really put a smile on my face and a laugh in my belly. What makes me happy? To share the gospel is my greatest joy. Paul used the word joy or rejoice 16 times in the book of Philippians. He was chained up 24-7 to someone when he ate, when he slept, when he went to the bathroom, and what does he say (Phil. 1:12), "but I want you know, brethren, that the things which happened to me have actually turned out for the furtherance of the gospel."

Dean

12/20/13

My Dearest Kathleen,

What a wonderful day I had with you today. A man once told me everything in life is lessons or blessings. When we learn our lesson, it turns into a blessing. One of my favorite scriptures is Song of Solomon (2:16). My beloved is mine, and I am his. In my previous life, BC (before Christ), I always considered you mine but not always the other way around. What a difference nine years makes. What a great feeling to belong to God first, along with you. I hope I am not putting the horse in front of the cart. I believe, when Christ is the focus of our relationship, failure is not an option when money doesn't matter, when possessions do not matter, when the only thing that matters are you and I, taking the gospel message to the ends of the earth. I heard a sermon the other day about redeeming the time.
I miss you; I want you; I love you.

Dean

Dec. 22, 2013

Dear Dean,

Suddenly, tonight, fear is overtaking me... Don't leave me... Please don't leave me again. I'm so frightened. I'm shaking and crying. I'm so scared of losing you. I'm not afraid of waiting. I'm afraid you'll get out and decide there are other choices. (Transparency, right? Honesty, right? I must tell you my fears so you can help me deal with them and reassure me.) You've called three times today, that should be reassurance enough... But my past has been filled with abandonment and rejection. I struggle with it still today.

In the last 9 years...I've been a peer-reviewer for educational journals, received eight grants, had seven articles published, one chapter in a book published, was hired as a consultant by an internationally prestigious testing company, was elected on the board of the International Board of Dyslexia, I presented at 11 competitive conferences, I presented at an additional 30 other events (school in services, service organizations, etc...), winner of the "teaching" award year at my university, winner of the doctoral student of the year... And guess what...I'm not that person since I got back from Africa. If anything I'm proud of...it's all the presentations with J.R. at the service organizations and churches about Africa (we've done 10 presentations together)... Now that's been cool. "I no longer need preeminence, prosperity, position, or promotion... I don't need to be recognized or rewarded...too little divine mission and dwarfed goals with cheap living."... ("Fellowship of the Unashamed"). I'm a kingdom seeker... It's sad to climb the corporate ladder, sacrifice so much, and get to the top to realize all I want is a tent, my husband, my God, and my kids. I don't know what the future holds...but I know who holds the future.

Kath

12/26/13

Dearest Kathleen,

When I first moved away, I had no TV and couldn't really pick up any radio at that place. I would sit there at night by myself, drinking myself blind and writing songs. I was so heartbroken; it would have saved everybody much heartache if I would have put down the bottle and picked up a Bible. I wrote this song...

Well, I wake up, in the morning
Still in love with you
Wondering do you, do you ever
Feel the way I do.
Then the sun breaks, as my hearts breaks
You told that we were through
Then I wake up, in the morning
Still in love with you.
Dean

12/28/2013

Dear Dean,

Tomorrow is our anniversary...a day I thought I had forgotten years ago. Why does it still hurt? I'm so hurt. I know you say, just say the word, and you'll tell everyone about us... But you must realize, by not telling people yet, I'm not just trying to protect me, I'm trying to protect you, and I'm trying to protect our kids. My family doesn't have the best impression of you... I want God to work on them, so you have a "fair chance" to show you have changed.

We are not in the situation because of me. This is not my fault. I'm really trying here; this is really hard. I mean really hard. I love you, and I'm trying. Your mom telling me after the divorce that there are two sides to every side of the story, and you're happier now...after our marriage ended. There are not two sides... There's only the truth (God's side). I know you're not that man anymore. I know that man is dead. I know, just as Christ died on the cross, "it is finished!" I know… So why does it all hurt so bad?

Father, please bring healing and peace. I feel like my heart is breaking. I can't breathe. My chest is caving in heavy. I feel so broken. I come broken to be mended. Rescue me, Lord, again. Restore me to a place of healing. Bring healing to our family. Bring restoration. These wounds still seep and bleed. Are you sure I can do this, Lord? Are you sure I'm strong enough now? Were there times Hosea collapsed and just claimed, God, I'm too broken…too shattered to pick up the pieces and trust you to try this again? Were there times Gomer just didn't know what to say to comfort her spouse in the healing process? Why do I have this feeling this is only the beginning… Are you sure, Father, we are up to this process?

Kath

12/31/13

Dearest Kathleen,

I, Dean, take you, Kathleen, to have and to hold, in sickness and in health, in richer and in poorer. I promise to love you just as Christ also loved the church and gave Himself for her. I promise to sustain your purity, never to put you in any compromising situations. I promise not to purposely anger you, and I promise to exalt, esteem, honor, and encourage you. Til death do us part. I love you, good night, sweetheart. With all my love, God bless and keep you.

Dean

1-4-2014

My Beloved Dean,

Your letter finally came at 3:00 p.m. this afternoon. I checked the mail three times today. I know the mail always comes around 3:00, but I was so hopeful it just might come sooner today. My cold is worse today. I've taken cold medicine all day and feel achy and can't quit coughing. I just feel so fatigued. But your letter was so wonderful; I read it again and again. I cherish every word and cling to it. It warms my heart. I adore you. I love you. This love is so great and better than any relationship I've ever had... I would rather have this...even this and wait for seven years than return to any day in my previous days. Your words bring me encouragement, love, and hope. In this letter, you had written the vows to me...the most precious vows I've ever read... words of promise from your heart. I only want God, you, and the boys.

So many times, I pleaded with God that I needed a man that had a vision like mine, that loved the Lord, that had a servant's heart, that would love the boys... That man was you; it always has been you... God was just preparing you for your return home and preparing me. And as I have mentioned numerous times, you were and still are the only man I have ever found sexy... You're the most attractive man I've ever met. You're the only one I desire.

Goodnight, Dean. I love you. I will wait for you.

Kath

1/26/14

My Dear, Sweet Kathleen,

How beautiful and wonderful you are. I am so excited to start my new life with you, and I am so excited that I will finish my life on this earth with you as well. The Mennonites came into the prison today and talked about an acronym LCES: look out, communicate, escape route, safety zone. The man talked about how this applies to our spiritual life as well. Look out: We always need to be on the lookout for Satan, for things that make us stumble. Communication: We need to stay in communication with God through prayer. Escape route: We always need to know that God is our spiritual escape, and he can get us out of situations that might make us stumble. Safety zone: We need to stay hooked up with strong fellow believers. With all that said, my point is, I'm learning about my spiritual weapons. I refuse to dabble in anything I know to be sin. When I get out, I will not be drinking, and, sweetheart, I won't care when you ask where I was and what I was doing.

I love you so much my friend, my love, my wife.

Dean

On Valentine's Day, Dean mailed me a Valentine's card. Inside he wrote these words:

2/14/2014

If tomorrow never comes, will you
know how much I love you
Did I try every way to show you every day
If tomorrow never comes.

The words were from a country song written by Garth Brooks (1989) that was sung at our wedding in 1990.

2/18/14

Hello sweetie,

I pray you're doing exceptionally well. Everything here tonight is about the same. Have I told you before, prison reminds me of the movie Groundhog's Day, all except I don't wake up to Sonny and Cher singing "I've Got You, Babe." I wrote to our friends Patty & James and told them the good, wonderful news of our reconciliation.

I love you, sweetheart. God bless and keep you.

Dean

Dean continued to call and write. Phone calls were recorded, expensive, and limited to twenty minutes, although we spoke a couple of times a week. We wrote letters weekly and, at times, multiple letters a week. I drove to the prison once a month to visit. The drive was long, four hours each way, but we were often permitted to visit six hours. I was allowed to enter with a roll of quarters. I would go over to the vending machine and purchase a cheese Danish. There was a microwave in the visiting room. I would heat the Danish. We would thank God for his blessings and share that meager Danish, like it was the finest meal. Each time, before I left, we would spend time in prayer for the boys. At times, those prayers made me feel as if the world stopped, and we were transported to another place. All the noise from the visitors' room would quiet, and in that moment, our hearts would pour out, united to God.

I was cautious not to share my personal life with people. I had yet to tell my parents that I was back in communication with Dean. I was sure they would not be in favor. They had witnessed my unhappiness for years and saw the effects of all the trauma on me and the boys. J.R. knew I was back with Dean, although I had not talked to Coy about it much. When I tried to talk to Coy about it, he simply responded, "J.R. and I are grown. What you do, Mom, is your business and doesn't involve us." I was quiet about it at work and had not shared with any friends. I spoke to my pastor, but even he seemed apprehensive. Dean still had multiple years left to serve in prison, eight years at the minimum if he got awarded "good time." There was something different about Dean. I could see Christ in him, and I was positive the change was authentic. I knew God was leading me back to my marriage. I was not sure what kind of marriage it would be with Dean incarcerated and me living on the outside. All I knew is that returning to my marriage was biblical, and I knew God would bless me for being obedient.

The letters and phone calls continued. By February, I had agreed to reenter my marriage. Dean and I could not legally remarry. Although there was a policy of the procedure to get married in the prison, the state denied obtaining the marriage certificate unless both parties were present. I traveled to the prison for a Saturday visit. There was no wedding dress, no wedding invitation, no announcements to family or friends. Dean had on clothes which looked like scrubs worn in the medical field, except the color was florescent orange. He wore a large, orange, short-sleeved shirt with a white undershirt. He had orange pants; those pants were so baggy on him. The pants had an elastic waist. To fit his tall length, he wore a 2XL. The pants were huge on him in the waist, butt, and thighs. The prison required closed-toes shoes. I wore a sports bra since underwires would set off the metal detectors and would require a search from the guards. I often commented that those sports bra made me look like I had one large "uniboob," far from attractive. I wore a sweater with jeans, no fancy earrings, no jewelry. The day was cold and brisk with snow flurries, like the snowy day we originally married twenty-four years prior. Eight years had passed since we divorced, and that day we made a commitment to each other once again.

We simply sat opposite each other at a small square table and renewed our vows to one another. There was no preacher, no witnesses, no formal ceremony, and no holding hands. Dean and I reentered our marriage in the eyes of God; it would be several years before we could legally remarry.

After the visit, guards would announce, "Time to go!" Visitors and inmates would be permitted to hug briefly and have a short kiss. I called those kisses kindergarten kisses, only a brief peck on the lips with guards watching. Then inmates would be escorted to one side of the visitor's room and await their turn to be patted down and searched prior to their return to the cells. Visitors would be taken to the opposite side of the room and follow the line exiting the prison. As I followed the visitor line toward the exit, my eyes filled with tears. Once again, I would leave him there. I glanced back over my shoulder and saw him watching me as I left.

Dean said the prison allowed the inmates to wear a wedding ring. I would be permitted to get him a ring, but it would have to go through the prison chaplain. I mailed a short letter and the ring to Chaplain Montoya.

2-26-14

Chaplain Montoya,

How wonderful that we serve a God that is still in the business of miracles of restoration! I'm still in awe that God could take a family and marriage as broken as ours and bring healing and restoration. The scriptures state that Satan comes like a thief in the night to steal and destroy, and years ago, he destroyed our family. However, the rest of that verse states, but he (God) comes to give life and give life abundantly. Dean and I are standing together as we take back the years Satan robbed from us. God promises to restore the years the "locus have eaten," and we stand in faith that God will restore to us the years we lost in "Egypt."

The enclosed ring is a symbol of my love to Dean, but more than that is a renewal of my com-

mitment to my marriage. It is a symbol for Dean to take his ordained place as the spiritual leader of our family. It is a symbol of celebration of restoration and the faithfulness of God. The ring is a C.J. Avery wedding band, which is in Hebrew. The Hebrew comes from the Song of Solomon, which reads, "I am my beloveds, and she is mine."

I appreciate your willingness to get this to Dean. Furthermore, I appreciate your willingness to stand in the gap with these men in the faith day in and day out.

Sincerely, Kathleen

The months that followed would be filled with work, letters, and phone calls. Once a month, I continued to travel to the prison. Since I lived miles away from my parents and the boys, no one knew of my once-a-month prison visits. I would leave early in the morning, before 5:00 a.m., and return home around 7:00 p.m. The visits were always stressful for me. Guards were rude and difficult. I noticed, with each visit, the lady that did the "check-in" paperwork became more and more obviously rude to me. On one visit, she commented how "cute" my headband looked. I thanked her. When I finished the paperwork, went through the metal detector, and was ready to go into the prison, she told me the visit was denied. When I questioned why, she stated, "You're out of dress code. Headbands are against the rule." I took the headband off and threw it in the trash. She took it out of the trash and made a comment about how much she liked the headband and how she was going to enjoy it. She then elaborated on Dean's "long fingers" (*What an odd comment*, I thought) and how "attractive he was." She mentioned how once a week, she went back and visited with him. By the time I reached the visitor's room, I was steaming mad. How dare she! I immediately told Dean the whole story. He said she was part of a church group that came in once a week in the evening. He truly did not know she was interested in him and had not returned the affection. She continued to make my visits difficult for many months to follow. Visits would be canceled due to prison lockdowns, bad weather, or other various reasons.

5/19/2014

Hey, Kath,

As you have more than likely realized by now, we are locked down for shakedown. Not cool, but it does give me time to write to the most beautiful woman in whole wide world. I would much rather use the phone and hear your voice; however, I am most thankful that I am able to correspond with you at all. The years we spent suffering are turning around. Praise God! I know God can and will deliver me from prison. I can't remember the last day I was able to call and talk with you.

Last night, I was trying to find a scripture for my roommate. I couldn't remember just where it was, but I remembered it was about redeeming the time. I found it this morning in Joel 2:21: "So I will restore to you the years the swarming locust had eaten, the crawling locust, the consuming locust, and the chewing locust."

Kath, I want to make it perfectly clear how much I love you. You are such an awesome woman of God. You are the one who makes me whole. Truly, you are flesh of my flesh and bone of my bone.

I love you, blessed woman of God!

Dean

6-1-14

My Dearest Dean,

I was hoping you were going to call after I got out of church. I always have so much I want to talk to you about. The sermon today was on Ephesians. During the sermon, Pastor Kelly talked about Moses and David committing murder. He talked about how God used these mighty men of God and how he had "chosen" them. The more he talked, the more I had tears. I know you are a David or a Moses...divinely chosen and gifted, not an "ordinary" Christian but a "peculiar" people and radical! I felt such confirmation in my spirit, a man after God's own heart with an incredible testimony of His goodness and grace.

I just realized I'm turning 48 this month. I've checked the math twice. All year I thought I was 48. This getting old thing is so confusing. It is ter-rible when you don't even know how old you are!!!! I know, I'm older than you...you were going to say it!!! Hahaha.

I love you always and forever and never have enough time to talk to you...

Kath

6/1/2014

Hello, my Darling Wife,

It is Sunday afternoon and the time I ought to be calling you and would love to do so. However, I am unable to do so because the phone has been turned off for the last couple of days. It's hard not to get upset with the guards. I need to keep reminding myself they are not the ones who put me here; I did. So if there's anyone to get upset with, it's me.

As I read through J.R.'s song, my heart broke. I had thought I was going to ride back into your life and save the day, that I would be the hero, and I figured everybody would be so happy I was home, and I would continue in my sin-filled life. There is a lesson here about being too late. Just a couple of months prior to me being locked up, you had asked me to come home; however, I thought there were too many strings attached. God calls us much the same way and in the same way, we think there are too many strings attached. We believe there is still too much fun to have, not realizing that the true fun is with God. Until one day we realize, and it is too late. I thank God that I have another chance. I have my regrets all the time. I missed ball games, graduations, laughing, and crying with you all. Oh, the years the swarming locust have eaten.

I love you, sweetheart, with all my love.

Dean

6/10/14

Hello sweetie,

I know how much you like letters, and I'm currently locked in this cell. So I thought I would just drop you a quick line, letting you know how much I love you, adore, admire, and want to spend the rest of my days with you.

I still can't understand how my love for you and the boys was so misguided. I had no clue what life was all about. I want to go home. I want to sit and talk to you about how good our God is. I want *to reassure you that it is till death do we part. I shouldn't have left. I will do better. Thank you so much for another chance. You're an awesome woman of God, and you're very good looking to boot.*

I just know God didn't bring us through this to be ordinary people. God called the children a peculiar people. I think you hit the nail on the head when you said radical. That's exactly who and how we need to be.

Dean

At the end of June, I finally told my parents about reuniting with Dean. My mom expressed how she had been praying for Dean all these years; however, she was clear to emphasize that it had been for "Dean's salvation and not for you to get back together." My dad had heard J.R. talk about Dean's conversion to Christ multiple times in recent years. My sister-in-law (Dean's sister and my brother's wife) had also talked about what a good Christian Dean was now. My dad was open to our reconciliation. If he had reservations, he held back and did not discuss it with me. Dean was happy that I finally agreed to tell the family. He was especially elated at how well my parents had received the news.

Dean called and told his parents. I think his mom was somewhat disappointed. She had assumed that when Dean got out of prison, he would come live with them. They lived in another town. She had waited years for her son to come home. Our reconciliation meant that Dean would get out of prison and come live with me. Dean did not tell me of her disappointment or comments, although I would hear from other family members. I was still bitter at his parents' actions when Dean went to prison. Years later, our relationship would be mended.

6/30/14

Dear Kath,

I'm so happy your folks took the news as well as they did. I can't imagine the tension that had to be hanging in the air as you broke the news to them. It was so good to hear that your mom had been praying for me. When you told me your dad said, "That's wonderful," I teared up when I heard those words on the phone. I'm such a crybaby. Your words, "I want to make it this time," are still echoing in my ears. I want to remind you of a poem you sent me from a Zimbabwe African Pastor: "I'm part of the fellowship of the unashamed. The die has been cast. I have stepped over the line. The decision has been made. I'm a disciple of His, and I won't look back, let up, slow down, back away, or be still." There are no problems too great, no circumstances too dire, mountains too high, valleys too low, no rivers to wide or deep, swift, or slow that cannot be overcome by the blood of Christ.

I love you, sweetheart, with all my love.

Dean

CHAPTER 11

A New Creation

Dean had been in Bible coursework through a Bible college the last two years. I found out that Dean had been in the exact same Bible program I was pursuing. He was enrolled in Bible school. I had only completed a few courses; Dean was at the end of his second year of coursework. Dean was being mentored by a local pastor, Brother R. Floyd, to fulfill the requirements of the internship/mentorship. I was volunteering with Pastor R. Floyd's brother (also a pastor, Brother T. Floyd) at a local children's home. Dean and I were hundreds of miles apart. I was in awe at the way God had orchestrated our lives. We were both in the exact same Bible school, learning the same coursework, and the two brothers were instrumental in both of our lives. Too many coincidences to be accidental, God was working behind the scenes of our lives the whole time. Furthermore, God was training us up in the same thought and biblical foundations. Dean lacked one year of completing the program for ordination.

Meanwhile, two investors had approached the state department of corrections and wanted to pay for cohorts of prisoners to go through seminary. These Christian real estate investors would pay the cost for a private Christian university. They would arrange with the university to send professors into the prison to teach in-person classes. The investors would travel to all the state prison institutions and handpick twenty-four men for the first cohort. These chosen inmates would be responsible for their own general education coursework through community colleges and/or universities; however, the investors would pay for the last two years of college courses in Bible/seminary coursework, and the inmates that complete would receive a bachelor's degree in pastoral studies. At the completion of the program, the inmates that completed the program would be sent out to various prisons throughout the state to infiltrate the prisons statewide.

Dean was chosen to be interviewed. He would later be notified that he was chosen for the program. The decision to leave his current prison was difficult for him. He was a shepherd to those men. He felt like he was abandoning them. However, even if he chose to stay in that prison, he could be transferred at any time without a say in the decision. Dean decided to accept the offer and was transferred to another prison, three hundred miles away from his current prison. He was enrolled and started the Biblical Studies Seminary Program.

The program was at a prison closer to my home, only a little over one hundred miles away. At the time of the interview or acceptance, Dean had no idea where he would be going; in fact, until deep in the process, he thought the program was being implemented at his current prison. I would be able to visit weekly on Saturdays. For that year, Dean and I enjoyed multiple visits. I became friends with some of the other prisoners' wives. I got used to seeing the same familiar faces. I exchanged phone numbers with other wives, and we would notify one another if we had any information, such as prison lockdown or messages from inmates to relay to their loved one. Many wives and family member relocate each time their loved one is transferred to a new prison. Many of these women I would see again and again through the years at multiple prisons. We got to know one another and would ask about the kids, the grandkids, and other topics. I never knew what their husbands were in for, and they never asked about mine; instead, we comforted each other, asking "How much longer?" or updates on their appeal or case.

This prison was not as difficult to visit; I did not have to go through the hand screening for drugs, metal detector, or searches. I rarely was turned away because the visiting room was too full, although I did arrive early to get my place in line. There were times the prison went on lockdown, and I could not go visit, but our visits were much more frequent than ever before. Letters were not as frequent since Dean would call on Sunday afternoons and sometimes on Tuesday nights, and we would visit in person on most Saturdays. I cherished our Saturday visits that year.

Before long, Christmas came and went. As with so many holidays before, we spent them apart. Rarely were there Christmas presents for each other. If there were, they were small tokens, such as a card or depositing money on his commissary account for food and phone calls. At one point, even cards, photos, and newspaper clippings were no longer allowed. The holiday was not full of presents under the tree, although there were some prisons that allowed the inmates to decorate the inmate pod. Dean would tell me of the talented artists and the transformation of the pod with paintings of Mary and Joseph, the Christ child, and the three wise men. One year, Dean arranged for me to bring home the large painting of the three wise men. The mural was done on a flat bedsheet. I still have the painting.

12/21/2015

Dear Kath,

I used to stay up all night, putting toys together for the boys before Christmas; now I'm up all night writing letters. I don't know how, but Christmas snuck up on me. I thought I had another week. I hope these letters get there in time for Christmas. I will stay up and get these letters in the mail in the morning.

I thought I would have a present for you by now. That too did not pan out, so sorry. What can I give the most important person in my life, my best friend, the one who has held my heart for over a quarter century, when I have nothing to offer but my words? So my words it will be.

It has been about two years since we have been back together. I never would have thought that I would still be in prison. It doesn't seem fair to you for me to have pursued our relationship with you while still in prison. Although I do feel for your situation, I will not apologize for my desires for you. At one time in my life, I would have thought the right thing to do would be to offer the option for you to move on; I have come to learn that is no option at all. The last line of our marriage vows that come to mind are 'til death do us part, and that is exactly how I see it, 'til death do us part.

I so appreciate everything you do for me. I can't thank you enough for the support, the kindness, and the love that you continue to show me day in and day out. I believe I would have to point to you as the example of a person living their faith, not only preaching the gospel but living the gospel. That is the message I try to convey, to not just talk about it but to be about it.

Remember that story I shared with you about giving my cookies away? In secret, I gave my cookies to another inmate; I put them on his bed. I waited for him to come out of his cell. I was sure he would know they were from me. But he never said anything about them. I wanted him to know I was the one who gave them, contrary the characteristics Jesus discussed in the beatitudes, something I still find difficult at times. Even when I picked up trash off the floor, I wanted somebody to know it was me. I know that is a lesson we can all learn.

I want to let you know you rock my world, and I'm so grateful and thankful for you. It tears me up when I'm not there with you when you need encour-

agement or me to hold you after a long day. I am yours, and you are mine. I will always love you.

Your husband now and forever,
Dean

Spring arrived, and the prison was going to have a special church service. Dean invited me to come, and I agreed. The prison had allowed the prison church to raise money, selling food items to inmates for the last year. These prisoners had worked hard to host a church banquet for the families. There were sodas, pizza, and cake. The inmates had paid for all these items from their fundraising. There would be a church service and then time for families to socialize.

There had been multiple times through the years that the prison hosted special events for the prisoners, events such as college graduations, church services, and family picnics. I had never attended, and neither had the boys. Dean went for years without any visitors at those special events. He would look among the visitors, only to find that none of his family had shown. He would talk to the boys and invite them; however, the boys knew my feelings toward Dean and would never even mention it to me. I did not find out about those events until years later. At one point, I found a letter from Dean that mentioned his associate degree graduation ceremony. He mentioned how he would have invited his mom and dad but was hopeful that the boys and I would attend. I never knew about the graduation ceremony. Dean wrote how he anxiously looked out in the crowd of visitors, and no one from his family was there. After graduation, he walked back to his cell, while the families visited. I can only imagine the hurt and the disappointment. There would be years where Dean had no visitors.

"I'm so thankful for Pastor," one inmate said. His arms covered in tattoos with a cross made from dental floss hanging around his neck.

"Your husband has done so much for my son." She gave me a hug.

"Pastor is a good man." He shook my hand and proceeded to a seat.

People kept approaching me, one right after another.

I watched Dean take the microphone. He welcomed the families. He grabbed a guitar and led the praise band, leading the congregation in worship. The first song was by Casting Crowns, "Praise You in This Storm." The inmates had their hands raised. I raised my hand and began to cry. I recalled those early months in our divorce and how I listened to that very song daily. Dean stopped singing in the microphone. His voice cracked; tears rolled down his face. He turned his back toward the crowd for a moment and gathered his composure. He returned to singing. I watched as these men worshipped with all their hearts. I was so moved in this environment, this place, with these men. I had often heard the saying, "The church is not the building but the people." Here, in this place, I saw the *church,* the body of Christ. Dean then brought a message. He preached with passion and conviction. My eyes filled with tears as I watched him preach. Who was this man?

During the banquet, one person after another would tell me how much Dean had helped them or their loved one in this place. The personal testimonies shared did not stop until it was time to leave. I was in awe at God's faithfulness. I clearly remembered crying out to God, "Lord, do whatever it takes, and save my family. Save my marriage. Save Dean. Protect my boys." I can remember feeling like that prayer had never been answered. Dean had become incarcerated, and we had divorced. Dean said that I prayed him into prison, and now, could I please pray him out?

He was a shepherd, a pastor to these men twenty-four hours a day, seven days a week. He was their pastor. He lived with them. He ate with them. He never left them. Dean had to be an example for Christ, a shepherd every day, all day. He had to rely on God completely.

Dean had a bracelet made for me; it has the scripture reference 1 Corinthians 7:16 woven into the bracelet: "For how do you know, O wife, whether you will save your husband? Or how do you know, O husband, whether you will save your wife?" Dean claimed

I saved him. When everything was lost, and he hit rock bottom, he knew where to turn. Years of praying, years of going to church alone with the boys, years of trying to talk to Dean—all those years were planting seeds. When the time was right, God brought the harvest. Galatians 6:9 states, "Let us not become weary in doing good, for at the proper time we will reap a harvest if we do not give up." God had saved Dean. Now God was using Dean to save others. Dean was planting seeds in prison, and God will bring the harvest.

CHAPTER 12

Answering the Call

In the spring, I went to women's weekend with *Kairos Outside. Kairos Prison Ministry* is an interdenominational ministry that aims to provide support to those incarcerated and their families. *Kairos Outside* is specifically for women that have been affected in some way from incarceration. I was able to develop friendship with a network of women that understood what it was like to have a family member incarcerated. I wished I had known about this organization earlier in my journey, for so many years I lived feeling like I was alone, and no one understood. During that weekend, God revealed to me that I was waiting. I was doing time with Dean, but I was free and on the outside. I was waiting for Dean to get out, then I would work in the ministry. I made a decision that weekend to follow Christ. I knew, as a disciple of Christ, I needed to count the cost, to take up my cross, and follow him (Luke 12:25–33). I didn't know exact what following Christ would be like for me; all I knew is that he was calling me to trust and follow him.

3/18/2016

Dear Dean,

I decided I better write your letter on the computer since it has been so long since we have talked, and writing by hand would take me forever. I can't imagine how difficult it must have been to be on lockdown as Coy is getting married, and J.R. is leaving for Egypt. Somehow, you survive missing it all. But during all those days and events, I often thought of you and thought about how difficult that must have been.

Coy's wedding was beautiful. The "officiate" judge was a believer and quoted I Cor. 13. He talked about keeping God in the marriage and said an amazing Christian prayer, blessing their marriage "in the name of Jesus."

J.R. did the most amazing "best man" toast I've ever heard. He "preached," brought back memories, and prayed! It was incredible! Wow, that kid has the gift of preaching! He used to get so nervous speaking in front of people when I took him with me to talk at all those churches and social clubs. One of my favorite lines was, "Coy convinced me that I could fly and jump off of haystacks, and much to my surprise but probably not yours, he convinced this gal to marry him." He quoted from Ecclesiastes and talked about the calling and role of a man and wife. He talked about how proud he was of the man Coy grew up to be. I was in tears!

I must admit that I was so disappointed about the lockdown. I was going to visit Thursday, spend the night at my friends, and visit again on Friday. Spring break and didn't even get to see you once.

Coy is counting down the months and is determined to leave the state. J.R. is already gone. It might be a good time to take a different job in the next year, put the house up for sale, and relocate. I'm not making any decisions right now, but maybe this summer might open something up for me. I do like being so close to my parents and to you.

*Hang in there. Remember, you have a sexy wife
that adores you and thinks you're handsome!*

*Love always,
Kath*

I left the university that year in May. I sought a job in full-time ministry. That May, I wrote in my prayer journal:

Lord, I need confirmation that you have called me to leave. I need your provision, intervention, and direction. I need you to order my steps and make my path clear. I'm anxious, tired, worn, and clearly afraid.

A friend of mine, T. Floyd, had taken the job as the executive director of a children's home (ranch) in Texas. They were looking for someone to tutor two girls that had just arrived in April. The girls were significantly behind academically, and the home was looking for a tutor for the summer. In addition, they needed an English language arts teacher for sixth through eighth grade for the school. The school was located on the property and was for the residents. I traveled down to Texas during spring break to meet the headmaster of the school, Mr. Inmon, that April and took the job to begin in June. I packed up my home, contracted a realtor to list my home for sale, got my dog and items that would fit in my car, and left the state.

Matthew 8:22 became literal for me: "Follow me, and let the dead bury their own dead." I had to miss my own grandmother's funeral. My grandmother Hagood was a spiritual warrior. She loved Jesus and served him her entire life. She had continued to write and pray for Dean even when we were divorced. I was expected at the children's ranch, and I knew she would concur that I leave and follow the call, missing her funeral. I was moving 537 miles away. Through prayer, I knew God was calling there. The kids at the ranch came from abandonment, neglect, and abuse.

My decision to abandon all and follow the call of Christ meant I would live 800 miles from my parents, 424 miles to my nearest son, and almost 500 miles from Dean (in his current prison). I had been blessed last year to be able to see Dean almost weekly that last year. At the minimum, I saw him monthly. Choosing to follow Christ meant that I would sacrifice seeing my family and visits with Dean. I would move away from all my friends. I would relocate to a different state at the age of forty-eight, a place I had never lived in before without any family or friends. I planned to travel back on Christmas break, spring break, and over the summer. The first few months, housing was provided by the ranch, but eventually I purchased a travel trailer. I moved into the fifth wheel camper. I would put most of my belongings in a storage unit.

I stayed at the children's ranch for two years. The first year, I taught English Language Arts (ELA) to middle schoolers. The second year, the ranch would ask me to take over as principal of the school. I completed administrative leadership coursework years prior and was a licensed administrator. I poured my heart into the kids and staff there. The residential director called me the kid whisperer. I knew that God had empowered me to work with these kids. In some ways, I understood their brokenness. Although I was far from family, I felt at home.

My own children were grown and had moved away. My life was full of kids—kids sneaking out, kids hiding snakes in backpacks, kids yelling, kids fighting, kids studying, kids worshipping, and kids coming to Christ. Not all the kids had family, but some had family they would go visit for breaks or holidays. We would pray over every child's name each time they left. We would pray for safety, protection, and their return. Without fail, each time, at least one child would not return. Each time, the staff and I would be devastated.

Many of the children there had been sexually abused not just the females but several of the males. Their self-esteem and self-image were destroyed. They often felt shame and guilt for their sexual past. Even though these children were minors, many felt the sexual abuse was their fault, a typical response of sex abuse victims.

I worked at various children's homes for ten years. One of the most difficult things to accept is when a child is first rescued; they are not usually thankful. Their self-esteem is low. They do not believe they are worthy of a better life. Children that are rescued often feel like those adults, who have taken them away from their situation or biological parent, are enemies and causing them harm. Somehow, there is comfort in their dysfunctional old life; they know what to expect or what not to expect. I have watched teenage young ladies and young men sabotage their new life on purpose to return to their old way of existing. I have gone after kids that have run away, found them, brought them back, only to have them run away again.

I am reminded of the story of Rahab in the Bible (Joshua 2). She was a prostitute (a harlot). She sold herself for money to gratify others' sexual lusts. In those times, Israel often had prostitutes. Rahab had two spies come to her. She hid them and protected them from harm. She recognized that these men knew the Lord God. She negotiated with the spies for protection, "I have dealt kindly with you, you also deal kindly with my father's house" (Joshua 2:12). Her entire family was spared from death when the armies of Joshua attacked. The most significant part of the story though is that this woman is used by God. She has a son, Boaz, and his story is told in the book of Ruth. She is in the direct bloodline, the genealogy of Christ Jesus. God chose Rahab to be in the bloodline of Jesus.

Rahab made a choice to work as a prostitute. Regardless, God chose her. I worked hard to communicate with the kids their value and worth. If God could restore and use Rahab, they too could be restored and used by God. In addition, most of these children did not choose to be used sexually. Even those that had consented, there were other factors involved. God rescued Rahab, and he could rescue them. The Ranch's motto was "taking kids from crisis to creation." Our mission was to rescue and restore these children of God. Mr. Inmon gave me a charm one year with a card that read, "rescuer of children" and stated how I was instrumental in "saving others by snatching them from the fire" (Jude 1:23). I knew my work; there was making a difference in the lives of kids. Even more so, I knew it was God's work, and I was just his instrument.

I traveled back for summer and fall break but was unable to see Dean; the prison was on lockdown. Dean would call on the phone on Sundays and Tuesday nights. We would write occasionally. I missed time with him. I was so disappointed that the prison locked down exactly on my time off from work. The sacrifice felt even more substantial. I tried to keep my gaze on Jesus, knowing that I was to stay the course.

8/26/16

Hey, Sweetie,

I don't know if you received any news from our state since you live out of state now. I learned from the television that somebody was killed here Sunday night or Monday morning. I don't know much more than that. I want to let you know I'm fine except for the fact that I miss you.

My mind drifts to the first time I held J.R. The first time I held J.R., I had just gotten back from out of state. You said, "Would you like to hold your son?" What a special moment!

Another memory I have crossing my mind lately is when Coy came in from school with a piece of wood in his hand. He said, "Dad, I have a present for you. I made it in shop today. It's a push stick so you don't cut your fingers off on the table saw."

Thank you, Kath, so much for second chances!

Love you,
Dean

10/2/16

My Darling Wife,

Hello, Sweetie. I pray everything is well with you. I'm not sure you'll get this letter before you make the trip. As you can guess, by the lack of phone calls, we are locked down again; this time, I believe it is statewide. I'm very tired of this nonsense. On 9/29, there was another incident where a guy got his face cut bad, maybe the lockdown has something to do with that?

I'm so ready to get on with our lives. I was thinking about you rescuing Pattycake (your dog). You're working at the children's ranch and rescuing those kids, and I got to thinking, What in the world did you ever see in me? I came up with somebody else to rescue, and I hope you really listen to me when I say thank you!

So you bought a travel trailer? How exciting! I perceive lots of use coming out of that, perhaps a traveling ministry?

Oh, by the way, sweetheart, I am very proud of you and the great job you are doing with those kids. Sometimes it is just knowing that somebody cares, whether you live or die, if you get out of prison, or you don't, to change somebody's entire life. Thank you for being who you are and letting God use you. Thank you for your love, for your devotion, and as of now, your kindergarten kisses.

Dean

2/6/2017

My Dearest Kath,

Hey, sweetie. I kept thinking this lockdown would soon be over; therefore, writing you would be futile. The lockdown is not over as you can see, so I want to apologize for not writing earlier. Things around here seem to get crazier by the moment. I've had enough of the cleaning job. Every day they interrupt my peace and quiet to go clean up toilets that have been stopped up. They didn't turn off the water to the cell so any time a neighbor flushes, it comes up through the toilet in the next cell. I don't mind working by any means; I'm not above anything. It is just day after day on plugged-up toilets is starting to chop my hide. The guy that is supposed to be helping me just stands there, talking all day.

Valentine's Day is quickly approaching, and they no longer give out cards. So that means I'm going to have to write all that mushy stuff in this letter. One of my favorite photos of us is the one where I have my hat on, my arm around you, and I'm looking off somewhere, like we need to go. You have on a blue shirt, I believe, and you are looking up at me. I have no idea what you are thinking, but you seem to have so much love in your gaze. Of all the things that I have messed up, the one I regret the most is taking advantage of the love you had for me. That's not going to happen again. I don't know how, but wait... I'll spend the rest of my life letting you know how wonderful you are. You are the only girl for me. I love you, always and forever.

Dean

12/13/2017

Hey, Sweetie,

It's really aggravating not being able to speak with you. I hope and pray everything is well. We are still lockdown for what I'm not sure; however, I do know God is in control and working everything out for good.

My reading this morning was through John 10, where Jesus was saying he is the good shepherd, not a hireling that runs when things get rough.

So Christmas is coming. They are giving us a hard time about mailing out Christmas cards (crazy). I want to tell you how much you mean to me, and besides Jesus, you are the best Christmas present ever, a perfect segue into happy anniversary, twenty-seven years, I believe; that's more than half our lives. You know how much I hate to promise, but I can confidently say without reservation, the second half will be better than the first. You are an awesome lady, Kath, and I am so proud to call you my better half, my friend, my helper, my lover, my wife.

You are my always and forever,
Dean

I did not even return home for Christmas that year. A sponsor paid for some of the residential girls (that had no family) to go on a Christmas cruise. In addition, the sponsor had paid for my fare. No one bothered to ask if I liked water, which I do not, or to ask if I struggled with motion sickness (remember all those vertigo spells). The announcement was made to the girls at the same time I was told. I didn't have it in my heart to crush their excitement; they had so many disappointments in their lives. Off we went to celebrate Christmas on a cruise and in Cozumel, Mexico. That year certainly did not feel like Christmas, but my heart was full of love from these precious girls. When I returned from the cruise, I found a Christmas card (my gift) from Dean had arrived.

12/25/2017

Dearest Kath,

I have been racking my brain, wondering what a poor prisoner could get for his beautiful wife for her birthday. So I went to a local painter and ordered this card. If I remember right, Fall is your favorite time of year, and Fall has not come to South Texas yet, so I thought I could send Fall to you. [The card had two painted birds in a tree with fall leaves of yellow and orange].

The next conundrum I find myself in is what to write on such a beautiful card that will, in some way, somehow, get maybe just a little close to me explaining how much you mean to me. Solomon described how lovely his beloved is by saying that she "has bird eyes, goat's hair, teeth like sheep, neck like a tower, and breast like fawns" (I supposed they were bouncing). What can I say? It worked for him.

I find your beautiful blue eyes more captivating than fire on a cold winter's night, warm and furious. Your hair, definitely not like goats, they stink! Your teeth and neck, not like sheep or goats. Your breasts, I know you don't have a "uniboob." I think what is important is that you rock my world, and I can't imagine life without you. I'm sorry you will get this card late; you can hang it on your Christmas tree next year.

By the way, the birds painted on the card are evening grosbeak; they mate for life.

With all my love, always and forever, your loving husband,
Dean

As my second year ended, I knew it was time to go back to my hometown. Dean had been transferred to a prison that was only twenty miles from my parents' home. Dean had three years left on his sentence. I had moved away from my hometown at the age of twenty-four; I was now going back twenty-eight years later. J.R. and his wife had given birth to a precious little boy. I was now a grandmother.

The executive director/headmaster of the ranch wrote me a reference letter, and I said tearful goodbyes. I felt like I was deserting the kids and the staff, but in my heart, I knew this season in my life was over. I began to look for a job that April and departed from the ranch in late June.

3/30/2018

To Whom it may concern:

It is with mixed emotions that I type this reference letter. Dr. Kathleen has been a wonderful part of our Children's Ranch family for two years. We would hate to see her leave. She and I have faced many tough battles educationally and professionally. Kathleen always handles these situations with a lot of measured response and grace.

More than anything, you should know that as a Christian, she walks the walk. She has a wonderful testimony and has pressed into the lives of our children, resulting in the salvation of a few, planting and watering seeds for many more. I have been proud that Kathleen taught for me and led the school for me. We will definitely feel the loss of her sweet spirit here.

Sincerely,
Mr. Inmon

CHAPTER 13

A Legal Marriage

I obtained a job at a Christian school with Calvary Chapel. I interviewed with Pastor Shaun. The interview focused on my walk with Christ far more than my education or experience. I was transparent about my messed-up past and Dean. Pastor Shaun was more concerned about my spiritual walk currently. He offered me a sixth-grade teaching position, and I accepted.

I moved back near my parents and only a few miles from the prison, where Dean had been transferred. He had completed the seminary program and was moved to be an inmate pastor. There he would serve as a pastor to the facility and to the MHTC (mental health treatment center) unit. Once again, I could visit and see him. I made a point to see him a couple times a week; I would drive to the prison after teaching school and visit for a couple of hours.

Dean and I had legally divorced and felt that even though we did not need the endorsement of the state, to follow the "laws of the land" was biblical. We wish to remarry legally. That decision took five years to finally accomplish. In our state, it was not permitted to obtain a marriage license without both parties being present and presenting identification at the county office. Even though prison policy in the state granted the inmates the right to marry, there was no way to obtain the marriage paperwork. Furthermore, the licensed pastor had to be on the approved list by the prison. I could not appeal to a court unless we were both in the same county. I consulted a lawyer, wrote state senators, called the state prison board, tried to bypass by seeking a license in two other states, all to no avail. I was frustrated that we both felt God was calling us back to a commitment, but to legalize that commitment seemed impossible. For the first time, Dean and I finally resided in the same county. Dean had been incarcerated in six prisons over the twelve years; he had been transferred to an area where I grew up. I knew it was the hand of God. I filed a petition with the court for judicial authority to obtain a marriage license.

8/20/2018

Your Honour,

We are petitioning the court to allow us to obtain a marriage license of an absent party. We married December 29, 1990. On November 18, 2005, we divorced. Dean became incarcerated in December 2006. Since that time, we have both changed immensely. We committed to living our lives for Christ. We reconciled with one another on November 24, 2013. We have children and grandchildren together. We dearly love each other. However, due to the restriction of both parties being present to apply for a marriage license, we have been unsuccessful in legally remarrying. We are pleading with the court to allow us the opportunity to legally reinstate our marriage by obtaining a marriage license with an absent party. We appreciate your sincere consideration.

Respectfully,
Kathleen

The judge granted my petition. There was a pastor, Pastor Andrew, that volunteered at the prison once-a-week preaching. He agreed to meet us at the prison and marry us. I was allowed to bring two witnesses in to sign the paperwork; however, they had to be on

Dean's approved visiting list. My parents agreed to stand as witnesses. When Dean was transferred to this facility, my parents applied to be on the visitors' list. Much to my surprise, they would go visit Dean monthly when I was at work. They had never been to a prison previously, and I was shocked they would endure the whole visiting ordeal. They reestablished a loving relationship with Dean. At one point, Dean would tell me that my dad was his best friend.

On that September day, I rushed out of school an hour early, checked into the prison with my parents, and stood with Dean. Pastor Andrew shared a short message on the institute of marriage. He asked us each to affirm by simply stating, "I do." The entire process was over in less than five minutes. I was casual about the whole process and shared with very few that we were remarried that day. I found the whole ordeal annoying. We had committed with God, and I found it just to be a legalized hoop. I did not dress up. There was no cake, no presents, no celebration, although I did feel victorious that we had finally been able to follow what we believed God was calling us to do for years. The details of what Pastor Andrew even said were just a blur, but then, Dean looked at my parents, "I want to apologize to you both. I did not treat Kath the way I should have, and I'm sorry." Dean then looked at me, "Kath, I want to read you something. Husbands, love your wives, just as Christ also loved the church and gave himself for her and that he might sanctify and cleanse her with the washing of water by the word, that he might present her to himself a glorious church, not having spot or wrinkle or any such thing but that she should be holy and without blemish. So husbands ought to love their own wives as their own bodies. he who loves his wife loves himself, for no one ever hated his own flesh but nourishes and cherishes it, just as the Lord does the church. For we are members of his body, of his flesh, and of his bones. For this reason, a man shall leave his father and mother and be joined to his wife, and the two shall become one flesh" (Ephesians 5:31). He continued, "Kath, I did not even know what love was before. I think it is impossible to love without Christ. I know my responsibilities this time."

The moment was so touching and so sincere. Suddenly, the "legalism" disappeared, and I knew that even the reconciliation was holy. No pomp and circumstance, no fancy clothes, just a sterile prison visiting room, where two people committed to serve God as one flesh.

CHAPTER 14

A Prisoner's Wife

I pulled up behind the last car in the row and turned off my vehicle. The sun was bright, ninety-five degrees outside. The row of cars parked in the dirt parallel to the prison. In this line, with windows down, we would wait. I counted quickly how many cars were in front of me to figure out if I joined the line in time to get into the prison today. This prison had twelve tables inside—only twelve tables. After they are filled, no more visitors can enter. Visits are in two-hour blocks twice a week. I watched as a car passed us and pulled to the gate, must be someone new. The regulars all know to wait in the dirt until the guard allows us to pull through. We would wait in this line up to an hour. Cars started honking, and people yelled at her; they want to make sure she did not cut the line. I started praying for her. I saw her talking to the guard and then turn around to park in the line. Surely, they all remember their first time. There is no manual that tells how to navigate prison visits. Every prison is different: different rules, different procedures, different dress codes, different visiting days. Reading the state prison website prior to visit does not help. Each prison makes up their own schedule and rules, and it does not matter what the official websites state.

Finally, the cars in front of me began to move. One by one, each one was stopped. Vehicle registration and insurance were checked. The vehicle was searched, and a valid driver's license was presented. Once inside the gate, I proceeded to the parking lot. I saw her. She looked lost, and I could see the fear in her eyes. She had no idea where to walk, how to enter the prison, what items are prohibited, and what to bring. I walked over to her and introduced myself. She glanced at the bag of quarters in my hand, exactly $20 in a quart-size ziplock bag. Visitors may enter with quarters to buy items from the vending machines. A bag of chips or a candy bar is a huge treat to prisoners.

When inside, the check-in guard asked for my ID. I had legally changed my name back to Tayler. The guard announced that I was not an approved visitor. I explained that Dean and I had remarried, and I changed my name from Donalson. He proceeded to tell me that there was no way that I got married to a prisoner. I proceeded to state that we had been married here in the prison visiting room the week prior. He told me I was a liar. I convinced him to call Dean's case worker and verify my story. After the phone call, the guard looked at me and told me, "Well, that was dumb. You will not get to come inside and consummate the marriage. What was the big hurry!" I tried to explain that Dean and I are Christians, and we wanted to marry and return to our marriage legally out of obedience to God. He shook his head and made additional derogatory comments under his breath. Once inside, I found the new visitor and gave her a handful of my quarters. When the visit was over, I waited to walk out with the new lady.

I recall my first few years entering prisons. After the visit, I exited the halls with the other visitors, avoiding eye contact and wiping away the tears. I got to the parking lot and vomited in the dirt before I got in the car for the four-hour drive home. I was thankful that I no longer was traumatized by the prison visits; I had been visiting prisons for thirteen years now. I never saw the new lady again. Visitation in prison is difficult; I understood why so many family members never came.

> To everything there is a season, A time for
> every purpose under heaven: A time to be born,
> and a time to die. A time to plant, and a time
> to pluck what is planted; A time to kill, and a

time to heal. A time to break down, and a time
to build up. A time to weep, and a time to laugh;
A time to mourn, and a time to dance; A time
to cast away stones, and a time to gather stones.
A time to embrace, and a time to refrain from
embracing. A time to gain, and a time to lose;
A time to keep, and a time to throw away. A
time to tear, and a time to sew; A time to keep
silent, and a time to speak. A time to love, and a
time to hate; a time of war, And a time of peace.
(Ecclesiastes 3:1–8)

A season of time, as the prisoner does their time, so does the
family. Could there possibly be a purpose in this season? As hard as
it is to understand, God's ways are not our ways. Isaiah 55:8 states,
"For my thoughts are not your thoughts neither are my ways your
ways, said the Lord." Could prison time be a blessing? My journey
over the last thirteen years had taught me that God cared enough
to give us prison time. What Satan meant for harm, God meant for
good (Genesis 50:20). I know one must wonder how good can come
from circumstances like these but God. I love that phrase "but God."
Ephesians 2:4 states, "But God, who is rich in mercy, because of His
great love with which He loved us, even when we were dead in trespasses, made us alive together with Christ (by grace you have been
saved)." Why prison? Because of his great love to save our family.

Thanksgiving Day arrived. I was thrilled that J.R., his wife, and
our grandchild were in the United States this year. They were at my
home, along with my parents and my uncle. I was up early, preparing
the Thanksgiving meal. Mom and Dad came over early. Mom was
in the kitchen, helping me with the cooking, when the phone rang. I
picked up the phone and saw it was a number I did not recognize. I
answered, "Hello." Pastor Ray was on the phone. He was the senior
pastor of the Calvary Chapel I attended. Although I knew him and
worked at the school, he and I had never had more than a brief conversation in passing. I couldn't imagine why he would be calling me,
much less on Thanksgiving morning.

"I would like to go see your husband at the prison. Could you make those arrangements?" he questioned.

"Of course," I responded.

After the Thanksgiving meal, my parents and uncle went home. The rest of us went to the prison to visit Dean. On Thanksgiving Day, families were permitted a two-hour visit, starting at 4:00 p.m.

In the prison visitor's room, we—my son J.R., his wife, our grandchild, Dean, and I—sat around a small, square table. Only five inmates had visitors so far; after all, it was Thanksgiving Day. I told Dean that Pastor Ray called and wanted to visit. Dean was as surprised as I was and said he would make the arrangements the following Monday. We sat playing with our grandson with building blocks, reminiscing about how this would be the last Thanksgiving Day we would celebrate in prison. On the table was a spread of food, one cheese Danish, and four different kinds of chips. The vending machines were often scarce of food and never any main dishes. Often the machine charged far more than the posted price, one just keeps adding money until the item finally drops. We had warmed the last Danish in a nearby microwave. Dean was just so grateful we were together. After thirteen years, we were finally counting down our final months.

More than anything in those moments, I wanted to put prison behind us. I desired to forget the past and never recall this detour in our lives. However, Revelation 12:11 states, "They triumphed over him by the blood of the Lamb and by the word of their testimony." I often say, "I never chose prison ministry. It was chosen for me." By God's grace, he used prison to save Dean, our marriage, and our family. In those moments, when I feel this detour was a wreck, I must remember that it was God's love that wrecked our lives to save our lives. Galatians 6:14 states, "But may I never boast about anything except the cross of our Lord Jesus." The message was far from "poor me" but a story of God's redeeming love.

As Dean and I transitioned to this new season in our lives, we knew God would continue to use us in prison ministry, not because of who we are but because of who he is and to offer encouragement and hope to others. Instead, we wished to communicate Mark 5:19:

"Go home to your family, and tell them everything the Lord has done for you and how merciful he has been." We wished to comfort others that are discouraged, incarcerated, or love those who are in prison (1 Thessalonians 5:11, 14). We wanted our story to reflect his story.

The arrangements were made, and Pastor Ray took his assistant, Pastor Jason, with him to visit Dean. They visited that December day, exactly thirteen years and two days after that dark December night. Later I found out that the pastors had gone to the prison to get to know Dean. They knew he would be getting out soon and worried about the recidivism rate. Dean shared with them what God was doing inside at the prison church. He shared his own testimony. Together the men prayed. I know it touched Dean's heart deeply that they came to see him. Dean was encouraged. Pastor Ray and Pastor Jason said they would send Dean books to read. They sent in several books: *Seven Steps to a Successful Marriage* (Ries), *Calvary Chapel Distinctives* (Smith), *Spiritual Leadership* (Oswald Sanders), *Philosophy of Ministry of Calvary Chapel* (Smith), and *Living Water* (Smith). Pastor Jason would later get me a copy of the *Seven Steps to a Successful Marriage* too. These men were vested in helping Dean to have a strong biblical foundation. Pastor Jason stated, "If the enemy attacks, it is often within the marriage." He wanted Dean and I to be solid. I was amazed at the difference with the hearts of these men. How different it was from the Pastor that announced "Satan had our family" years prior. At this church, I didn't wear a scarlet letter of shame, and they even went to visit the prisoner. Later, the pastors would share with me that Dean looked thin and not well. They claimed, during the visit, that he was anxious and would often look behind him. They wondered if he was using drugs. Dean was sober. Those behaviors were manifestations of prison life. Dean did not know these men; I'm sure he must have felt uneasy. In addition, Dean explained to me that "those visitors were his, and it was his responsibility to protect them," thus he kept vigilant, watching every move in the room.

Another Christmas came. Another wedding anniversary passed. Just as so many holidays, time continued to pass. Dean mailed me a Christmas card. Inside he had written the following:

My very Dear wife Kathleen,

I pray this is the last Christmas/anniversary card I ever sent to you from prison. It has been another year apart from you. I have never felt closer to you. The word of God tells us in Psalm 133, "Behold, how pleasant it is for the brethren to dwell in unity!" I know that we are not brethren, but it is very pleasant for a husband and wife to dwell in unity. So as we push through another Christmas/anniversary season, let's not concentrate on what we do not have, but let's count our many blessings on what we do have.

I love you, sweetheart, always and forever.
Dean

CHAPTER 15

A Season of Waiting

Elijah fasted for forty days in the wilderness (1 Kings 19:8). During the flood, it rained for forty days and forty nights (Genesis 7:4). Noah sent out a dove after waiting forty days (Genesis 8:3–8). Moses spent forty days and nights on Mount Sinai (Exodus 24:18). Jesus spent forty days fasting in the desert (Matthew 4:1–2). After the resurrection, Jesus spent forty days on earth (Acts 1:3).

I felt the significance of forty days. Throughout the day, I was explicitly aware, there were 40 days remaining. After 4,678 days, only 40 days remained. I found it hard to even grasp the reality. Is this how the father of the prodigal son felt? "Bring out the best robe and put it on him and put a ring on his hand and sandals on his feet. And bring the fatted calf here and kill it, and let us eat and be merry, for this my son was dead and is alive again, he was lost and is found" (Luke 15:22–24). My husband, who was gone for over thirteen years, was coming home. Dean was going to be out prior to his sixteen-year sentence for a good time and for his education lump sum credits. He put his marriage ring on his hand. Let us eat red chili enchiladas (Dean's food request) and be merry.

The reunion and celebration were not as the father had planned (the parable of the prodigal son). The older son was jealous and bitter; "he was angry and would not go in" (Luke 15:28). I can just imagine the heartbreak of the father. His younger son has returned (what a moment of rejoicing), but the older son would not join in the celebration. In fact, he would not even greet his brother. Instead, the older brother brings up the past behavior of his sibling. He "devoured your livelihood with harlots" (Luke 15:30). The younger brother had changed. He repented, "Father, I have sinned against heaven and before you" (Luke 15:18). The older brother did not offer forgiveness. I wonder, did the brothers ever restore their relationship? I wish there was more to the parable. The father responded, at the end of the story, simply by saying that rejoicing was totally appropriate. "It was right that we should make merry and be glad, for your brother was dead and is alive again, and was lost and is found" (Luke 15:32).

"If you go back to Dean, I'll never speak to you again," she said. Surely, she did not mean that statement. Laquisha was my closest friend. After all, she was leading a Christian group to help individuals dealing with divorce. The main theme of the program was forgiveness and reconciliation when possible. She had been there for me through my divorce and before that, with me through crying nights due to Dean's behavior. I knew she just wanted to protect me. Dean was a different person after accepting Christ in prison. Dean was repentant. The friendship ended. I tried to say goodbye before I moved away; she never answered my calls.

"If Kathy decides to go back with Dean, that is it! I'm done," stated my sister Kay. How it broke my heart that as much as I loved her and wanted a relationship, much of her bitterness toward me was due to my faith and my choice to forgive Dean. She too was just trying to protect me. I had little interaction with her since Coy's high school graduation. There had been dissention among us for years, and how my heart longed to have her in my life. Somehow, I always managed to hurt her feelings. Dad told me what she said.

"I do not want to see him. You are welcome here, but don't bring him," stated my son Coy. I know so much of his response is due to the hurt and unresolved emotions. He had chosen not to get to know the new Dean. When a man comes to Christ, he is a new creation, and the old is passed away (2 Corinthians 5:17). According to my son, forgiveness was a weakness. He was verbal that he did not believe people could change. Coy had worked years in the police force; he had witnessed the worst in people. He did not want Dean around his family. He stated that only time would tell if Dean had really changed. He and his wife were expecting their first child.

My heart was broken. I cried for days. Was I to choose between my husband and my son, my friend, and my sister? I knew the scriptures; I was to cling to my husband, and we were one. As much as it broke my heart, where Dean was not welcomed, I would not go.

Jesus fasted and prayed for forty days; Satan came to attack. As we were at forty days, the attacks multiplied. I chose to celebrate. It is right that I should be merry and glad, for my husband, who was dead in sin, is alive in Christ! God had reconciled our marriage. Dean was finally coming home. I would rejoice!

I waited anxiously for the parole officers to arrive. Finally, they pulled up in an unmarked SUV. I opened the door and invited them to have a seat. They refused and stood as I sat down. They briefly went over their expectations. I asked them to wait as I grabbed a pen to jot down the rules. The one officer continued, "Do you know his charges?" In my mind, I was thinking, *You mean his charges thirteen years ago?* His record in prison of never having a write-up, completing college degrees and programs, being a mentor, a tutor, and a pastor were not mentioned. The parole officer only spoke of Dean's mistakes, his sin, him falling short of society's expectations. For the next two years, they would watch Dean. They would search our home, demand random drug and alcohol testing, require counseling, the list went on and on. I felt as if I was going to vomit. Obviously, the debt was not paid, and Dean would continue to reap the consequences of the December night so long ago. Furthermore, I would have my bedroom, home, and refrigerator searched upon demand. I certainly had nothing to hide, but the invasion of any privacy or trust was daunting.

Meanwhile, Dean faced the parole board in prison. His experience would not be much different. They would not mention the numerous college degrees he completed, his record, or the good he did for others in prison. One lady on the parole board would question him, "So what happened that night?" He would feel as if he was on trial again. Any response could make things worse. He tried to remain silent and just accept the story the way she told it, regardless of the truth. "So is that what happened in a nutshell?" she asked. "And this lady, Kathleen, she married you when you were in prison? She must be stupid!"

Dean tried to explain we were married for almost sixteen years prior to prison and reconciled.

"Why would she do that?" she exclaimed.

Dean simply responded, "She forgave me."

No matter what Dean did, it was not good enough. The experience reminded me of Paul's writing in the book of Romans: "There is no one righteous, not even one" (Romans 3:9–10). We are all guilty and fall short (Romans 3:23). We have all sinned (Romans 6:23). Even those parole officers fall short (although it was not advisable that I tell them that fact). Dean was guilty, but he is made righteous through faith in Jesus Christ (Romans 3:22). I am guilty. All the good I believe I have done for Christ—I still fall short. I am righteous only because of the cross, only because God gave his son to die for my sins (Romans 5:8). More importantly than me forgiving Dean is that God forgave him. The debt had been paid.

"Are you excited?" What an odd question that was for me. So many people asked the same thing. What is worse is that I didn't know how I felt. I didn't see Dean that Wednesday; the prison went on lock down with no visitors. I was able to get in for a visit on Thursday. The look in his eyes told me something was wrong.

"They changed the date, Kath," he said.

"Absolutely not!" I replied. I had already arranged to be off work, set up an appointment for Dean, planned the lunch, and J.R. and his family were coming—not again, no explanation, no understandable reason, just a new release date.

I drove home dazed. I lost hope. I had lost count on how many times we thought Dean would be released. I turned off the phone and withdrew. I was so hurt; I couldn't even talk. Friends and family tried to call and left messages. I just wanted to stay in bed. After three days, I sat down and wrote a song on the piano, trying to process my feelings.

Time Wasted

1.   *The kids are now grown*
From a broken home
There would be many times
I would lose all hope

2.   *Crying out to God*
When I could no longer stand
Trusting day by day
That he had a plan

Chorus:
All the years we wasted
All the time we lost
There would come a time
We would count the cost

3.   *So let's start all over again*
Let's extend our hands
Offer mercy and grace
Let forgiveness fill this place

4.   *So let's start all over again*
Take the time to pray
Kneel on bended knee
And lift our hands in praise

Chorus

I didn't know what I was supposed to be feeling; I only knew what a struggle and trigger the last few days had been. A time that was supposed to be a reunion and rejoicing was full of emotional turmoil for me. We lost over thirteen years. Our kids were raised in a broken home and without a dad present. The effects of those events left scars.

Suddenly, I felt like I was being hit by a freight train. I had migraines. I was emotionally and physically exhausted. On the weekend, I ended up missing an event that I had made a verbal commitment to be there, but my migraine was so bad, I was nauseous and unable to go. I wished so desperately I could just forget the years prior to prison and the years in prison. No little girl dreams of growing up and being the wife of a prisoner. I find it hard to write even now without tears rolling down my face.

When Dean and I married, a huge snowstorm blew in the day of the wedding. The photographer, most of my relatives, and many friends could not make it due to the bad road conditions. We had to stop short of our honeymoon destination and stay in a hotel for several days due to the bad weather. I certainly had not planned to get married in a snow blizzard.

One must wonder if it is better to have no expectations. I felt like that twenty-four-year-old bride looking out the window at the snowstorm.

John Piper (2019) wrote, "Occasionally, weep deeply over the life you hoped would be. Grieve the losses. Then wash your face. Trust God. And embrace the life you have."

When Jesus rose from the grave, the scars on hands and in his side remained. Perhaps, the problem is not the scars but me trying to hide them. With the pressure of social media, we have become a "perfect" society, and we hide our struggles and disappointments. I was living a life I never dreamed of living, a life of disappointments, but also blessings I could never have imagined: a marriage reconciled and grandbabies.

My teacher peers and classroom parents threw a "welcome home" shower for me and Dean. I was so surprised. Dean was speechless and choked up when I told him on the phone. They included clothing, gift cards for clothes, meal gift cards, movie cards, and sweet treats. The life I had was full of Christian sisters that showed me God's love. I decided to embrace the life I had, scars, and blessings. I made a vow to count my blessings as I waited.

I recall my previous places of employment. Most of my peers did not even know I had a husband in prison. I confided once to one peer that my husband was in prison, and she responded, "You better keep that a secret. If people in the community know, they will never accept you." We never spoke about it again; in fact, I never spoke about it again. I had spent years hiding Dean's incarceration. I had peers at work try to set me up on dates or introduce me to male friends. My own grandmother with Alzheimer's kept forgetting that Dean and I had reconciled, and telling the story again and again only brought her shock and trauma. When she would ask if I was dating anyone, I would simply respond, "No, Grandma."

"Well, you need a man. A woman has needs," she would say. I would quickly change the subject, and she would forget what we were discussing.

Once, when teaching at the university, my graduate students were visiting before class. I was organizing my materials on the podium, getting ready to go live on the broadcast camera. The class was for teachers working on their masters' degrees; some students were in person, while multiple students were at a distance at various sites. I was the professor of the class. "He is just a problem. His dad is in prison, and his mom is always gone and doesn't care. No one helps him with homework. What do they expect? I can't make him learn or behave. Consider his family."

Another teacher joined in, "I know, I have a kid in class just like him. His dad is in prison too."

The TV screen started flashing "Live."

"Welcome to class," I began. I found it so hard to gather my thoughts. Overhearing that conversation between those two teachers rattled me to the core. It was so difficult for me to focus. Their conversation broke my heart and infuriated me. "Those families," "those kids"—I was one of "those families." Do those families look like their professor or the banker or their hairdresser?

Calvary Chapel was different. I didn't hide my past or Dean's incarceration. My peers knew. The pastors knew. Several parents of the kids I taught knew. My headmaster (principal) knew. I didn't have to live in secret and shame. In fact, I disclosed my messed-up past on my application, Dean in prison, and even my marriage to Leslie. My headmaster, Pastor Shaun, has always demonstrated God's love to me, the staff, the families, and the children. His spiritual leadership taught me more than he will ever realize. There were certainly those few that judged me or Dean, but those encounters were rare rather than the norm.

CHAPTER 16

Coming Home

I wanted everything to be perfect. As the day came closer, there seemed to be more things unfinished. The night before, I rushed around mopping quickly. As I mopped the bathroom, somehow I hit the lid of the tank on the toilet; it cracked and broke. I picked up the broken piece. I rushed to Home Depot and to Lowes; no one sold the toilet tank lids, although they could be ordered. I rushed back home. At this time, it was already ten o'clock at night. I used Gorilla Glue, trying to put the piece back on, only to have it fall and break in another piece. After hours of gluing the counter, my fingers, and the lid, it held together—a shattered, broken mess. I rushed to mop the last room, only to slip on the wet floor and crash onto a child safety gate, a huge strip of a black bruise would adorn my back side by morning. All the rushing, all the preparing, and the house, and I was a mess. Several sleepless nights, so much left undone, and still all the cooking to do to make Dean's favorite meals—he would be home to find a bruise, exhausted wife, and a pan full of burnt biscuits.

The whole ordeal reminded me of a story in the Bible about a woman named Martha. Once again, I had successfully become Martha, rushing around. He would come home to a house full of company (family), and I would be busy in the kitchen, serving everyone, when what my soul needed was for everyone to leave and let me sit in silence with my husband.

The story in the Bible (Luke 10) of Mary and Martha has always puzzled me. Perhaps the story frustrates me because I too am so much like Martha. After all, with all the company, what was Martha to do? Someone surely had to prepare the meals, prepare the house, and deal with all the company. I can so hear the tone in Martha's voice when she stated, "Lord, don't you care that my sister has left me to do all the work by myself? Tell her to help me!" Part of me believes that Martha would sit down and soak in that precious time with the Savior if everyone would just leave. Thus I found myself bitter and longing for everyone to just leave and give me time with my husband.

Just as the company all wanted to see Jesus, the family all wanted time with Dean. Furthermore, he wanted time with all of them. Jealousy and selfishness are not becoming attributes in me; I had set up so many expectations of what his coming home would look like, and the next week would lead to much disappointment. We would rush around in a daze of obligations, appointments, and company.

I was so excited to pick Dean up from the prison. My Kairos sister Linda had warned me to bring loose-fitting clothes, like sweatpants. Linda had a son do time in prison. Dean insisted that his size had not changed and to bring his Wrangler jeans. I questioned how he knew if his size changed, after all, he had just worn loose fitting pants, like scrubs, for years, and it is not like they used a tape measure or weighed him. He wanted his jeans and boots. We waited a couple of hours for the paperwork to be completed. He walked out in jeans and his boots (walking stiffly in the tightest wranglers I have ever seen). I wondered how he was going to bend down to get in the car without splitting those pants. I had some family gather at the house and cooked all his favorite foods. When we left the prison, we had to report immediately to the parole office. It would be more than six hours before we would be home. I should have never planned to have a "welcome home" gathering on release day.

We left the prison and drove straight to the parole office (as mandated). We left the parole office straight to the motor vehicle department (MVD). We were told Dean needed to get an ID since there was an expiration on his formal release prison identification card. Dean's case worker had reassured us that everyone would accept the identification card to obtain documents and needed identification. MVD would not take the state released prisoner ID, never mind the labeling of having to go to each office and verbally announce that he was a released prisoner. The MVD representative explained, "You need utility bills in the last sixty days." Dean calmly responded, and I asked how it was possible to get the needed documents. We drove back to the parole office. The officer wrote a letter asking for identification (ID) and stated Dean's address. We returned to MVD with the letter and a certified copy of our marriage license. The MVD representative explained that a "nonreal" ID could be issued, but he needed to see Dean's Social Security card.

These issues were just the beginning. He exited prison without a birth certificate or a Social Security card. His only identification was a prison release photo ID, and now an MVD "nonreal" ID. Social Security refused to acknowledge the prison ID or the driver's license as official government forms of ID. They informed us to bring in utility bills or copies of taxes. "Really? From thirteen years ago?" was my response. We went to the water company: "You can't add your husband to the bill unless he is on the taxes." We went to the tax office: "You can't add your husband to the taxes unless he is on the deed." We went to the county to add him to the deed: "You must have the deed amended and notarized. We no longer take documents from title companies to do that process, so you'll need to get a lawyer to do the paperwork." So in circles we went for almost four weeks. We finally obtained a Social Security (SS) card with Dean's last name spelled incorrectly, even though Dean had previously had a Social Security card with it spelled correctly and had paid into social security with previous jobs. She claimed his official birth certificate (which we did not have) spelled his last name differently.

Exhausted and frustrated, we finally arrived at the house to eat with the family. Dean sat quietly, picked up his fork, and stared. The family all started eating, and he remained frozen, staring at his fork. I finally whispered, "Are you okay?"

He looked up and responded, "I haven't held a fork for thirteen years." He held it with his fingers and continued to gaze. In prison, only small plastic sporks were provided. I was reminded of the scene in *The Little Mermaid* (Disney 1989), where Ariel finds a fork. She is told it is a *Dinglehopper*, and she cherishes the folk like a precious treasure. Here was Dean, staring at a fork, a *Dinglehopper*, like it was the most amazing thing on earth.

While some would ask, "How's the honeymoon going?" I would feel like we were having a honeymoon with grown children, my parents, and our grandchild. While I dearly loved all this family, what I needed the most that week was time alone with Dean. I found my attitude shifting, tension building, and anxiety. I reflected to find that my daily time with Jesus had been absent. My daily devotions had suffered greatly, my studying of the Word was nonexistent. The Martha in me had depleted me. I needed some quiet time, time to read the Word, time to pray, time to reflect, time to just sit at the feet of Jesus.

I rushed about task-oriented, preparing for Dean to come home. I'm afraid Dean would return home to find a bruised, exhausted bride. The Bible advises the believer to be ready for the return of Christ. Would Christ, too, return only to find me an exhausted bride rushing about? "Take my yoke upon you and learn of me…ye shall find rest for your souls. For my yoke is easy, and my burden is light" (Matthew 11:29–30). Mary longed and craved that time with Jesus. She did not seem to care that the obligations of this world were spinning around her, a dazed bride just wanting and fighting for those moments. Quite convicting as I reflected, did I crave time alone with Jesus like I craved that time with Dean?

Dean put in multiple job applications, but with the COVID virus just starting and with a felony, he only got one interview in which their response was, "we wouldn't have anything for you." Even an acquaintance from church who owned a business wouldn't hire him or even interview him. I was so worried about meeting parole requirements with finding a job or getting his driver's license. The world was full of challenges, and we continued to hit brick walls. Dean did remodel jobs for my parents and for a local pastor in town. I put the house up for sale, and we moved to a less expense home.

I went on walks with my dogs just to get out of the house and pray and sometime cry. I prayed for God to make a way when I couldn't find a way. I knew from the Bible that God loved me and loved Dean; I knew God wanted the best for us.

I returned home one evening from teaching school. Dean was frustrated. He had tried to help by cleaning the house but could not figure out how to turn on the dishwasher.

"Where is the dial?" he asked. "The old dishwasher had a big dial on the front." The small buttons could only be seen if the dishwasher was open, located on the edge of the machine, which was hidden by the kitchen countertop when closed.

Dean had never seen a keyless ignition on a car. He couldn't figure out how to start the car. I took him with me to an eye appointment. Due to the start of COVID, he could not go in with me. He returned to the car. That day in March was cold; he had not even been out for a month. He wanted to start the car to run the heat. Keyless ignitions require that one that pushes the break and then a button. Dean was sitting in the passenger seat, frozen and frustrated by the time I returned.

Little did I know, within a month, the world was about to become so different than the life I knew. COVID outbreaks hit, and our government shut down businesses, schools, gyms, churches, and restaurants. At times, I felt Dean adjusted much better than me during this time. When I referred to this world on lockdown, he just chuckled and responded, "This is not lockdown." I was frustrated at all the restriction, but Dean adapted easily to this way of life. Dean knew a life of lockdowns.

I was teaching school from home due to school closures with COVID. This circumstance gave me time with Dean at home to help him now with his adjustment to life on the outside. Parole let up on the job requirement during COVID, which gave us more time to pray and look for work for him. His parole officer was terrified of the virus, so he did not do home inspections or even require Dean to report in person. Dean spent hours reading the Bible and praying. I was worried about him, but he was clinging to God, and I found peace in that, knowing somehow everything would be all right. He had no friends; his friends were all in prison. He had family, but due to parole travel restrictions, he couldn't leave the county to see them. It would be over a year before we would be able to travel, and he would even see his oldest son, Coy, meet his daughter-in-law, and meet his grandson.

The parole board had mandated several criteria. Some of those included in the order of parole were the following:

1. Reporting monthly to the parole officer, which also included monthly fees.
2. No changing residence without permission. No outside cameras at residence.
3. Community service hours.
4. Obtain verifiable employment.
5. Attend anger management counseling.
6. Blow in an alcohol monitor machine four times that were designated daily.
7. No traveling outside the county without a travel pass.

The recidivism rate in NM is 57 percent, the fourth highest in the country. Recidivism refers to those that return to prison for any reason: could be reoffending but could also be parole violations. Those numbers scared me. I had to put my trust in God. These things were out of my control. We heard from other people that they struggled to obtain identification for up to three months. How in the world can these men meet parole requirements to have a job within a certain number of days when they cannot obtain identification to drive or obtain a job?

He slept in our bed like a tin soldier on his side, never moving. During his first week home, our dog barked. He sprung from the bed. By the time I sat up, he was already standing against the wall with his arm drawn back and his hand in a fist. A similar response happened every time I accidentally touched him in bed when sleeping. I had to put a large body pillow between us at night and be very caution to not touch him in his sleep. He was hypervigilant at restaurants or in public places, always watching every movement around us and only sitting with his back to the wall to be able to see all activity. He had come home with *post-traumatic stress disorder* (PTSD), like a soldier that had been gone to war. Prison life had made him adapt to behaviors I was not used to, nor did I understand.

I was reminded of the Christmas movie *Elf.* When I would take Dean out, he would run to hold the door open to everyone, wave enthusiastically, and try to talk to everyone. I saw people walking the long way around, trying to avoid the man they obviously thought was odd. I tried to talk to him about how his behavior was being perceived, but he could not understand. He would make eye contact and talk to everyone. He had lived in a community where he knew everyone. I lived in a neighborhood where I only knew a couple of neighbors and wore earbuds at the gym, talking to no one.

I had the preconceived notion that our life would go back to the way it was prior to prison, but this would take time. We only had brief hugs or a short kiss for years in prison visiting rooms; I used to call them kindergarten kisses. I thought of how wonderful it would be when he got home, and we could touch each other without rules and guards watching. However, he had become used to not being touched for years.

He stacked his shoes in rows under his bed. When I cleaned, I would move the shoes all back to his spacious closet. To this day, he continues to take his shoes and stack them in rows under his bed.

One morning, I was standing in the bedroom and saw him get in the shower. He walked in with his underwear on and proceeded to shower. He then washed his undergarment and hung it over the shower to dry. He saw me watching. I gently responded, "I can wash those in the washing machine."

He shook his head, "I know. I'm stupid."

Even J.R. commented to me one day, "Dad is different."

Dean would sit staring off in the distance in a daze. J.R., one day when talking to his dad, stated bluntly, "I'm talking to you. Do you hear me? I'm not talking to myself." Dean then responded.

Every decision, every move he made, whether he went outside, all these things were decided for him for years. Every morning, getting dressed was a big task for Dean. I would find him standing in his closet, staring at his clothes. He would be unable to decide which shirt to wear; there were too many choices. The inability to make simple decisions lasted months. He was used to going to the bathroom with permission. He would stand with his legs apart and put his hands behind his back, all behaviors done automatically without thought. He was acculturated to a different world than mine.

Dean would have to attend anger management counseling. He had been a pastor in prison for years and had no anger episodes. The mandate from the parole board seemed so random and uncharacteristic of Dean. He spent most of his counseling sessions witnessing to his counselor and encouraging her through her personal trials.

He would carry his alcohol monitor everywhere. An alarm would go off, and Dean would have to blow in the monitor. The monitor was set to go off exactly during the Sunday morning church service. Dean had not had a drink in over thirteen years. Once we obtained a travel pass to go see his parents. An hour outside of town, we realized that the alcohol monitor was left at home. Sweat beads rolled off Dean's face as we quickly turned around and headed home. I frantically prayed that we would get home in time for Dean to blow in the monitor. Any violation could mean a return to prison. We made it home as the alarm was sounding. Dean quickly blew in the monitor. Dean remained on probation for two years.

Jesus spoke of times of trouble and tribulation. In John 16:33b, he stated, "In the world you will have tribulation; but be of good cheer, I have overcome the world." In Nahum 1:7, the scriptures state, "The Lord is good, a strong hold in the day of trouble." Psalm 46:1 states, "God is our refuge and strength, an ever-present help in trouble." Psalm 59:16 states, "My refuge in times of trouble." Psalm 50:15 states, "Call on me in the day of trouble."

One day, during the COVID lockdown, Dean and I decided to climb the hill near the prison. The hill did not look that steep at the beginning of the walk. As we continued to climb, my legs felt the strain, and my lungs felt heavy trying to breath enough air. Dean walked in front of me without straining. We continued to climb. At the top of the hill, we looked down at the prison. Down the hill was the very facility he had spent the last two years of his sentence.

"I would look at this hill when I was in prison and say, 'Someday I'm going to climb that hill,'" Dean stated. Arms stretched out, I prayed for the guys that remained inside and for their families. I remember the months I drove past that facility when Dean was inside; I would pray for him each time I passed on the interstate. This time, Dean was out, but many more remained.

There was something serene in that moment. Looking down at the razor fencing and the bars on the windows, a place that once held Dean captive, now he stood above it as a freeman. I reflected on my own life, times in the valley, where freedom seemed so far away; at times freedom even seemed impossible—freedom from a failing marriage, freedom from a bad job, freedom from depression, freedom from addiction of alcoholism in our home, freedom from prison for Dean. Freedom.

I often have been held captive, even though physical bars did not restrain me. The psalmist wrote in Psalm 116:16, "You have loosed my bonds," and in Psalm 142, "Bring my soul out of prison, that I might praise your name." While many references in the Bible refer literally to "setting the captives free" (Isaiah 61:1; Luke 4:18). Being a captive can be physical, mental, emotional, and/or spiritual bondage—bondage, to be a slave. At times, I have even felt like a slave to email and cell phone messages. Thus I greatly enjoy turning off the phone and shutting down the computer and being out of reach. Jesus would depart from the people to find time alone to pray (Luke 4; Mark 6; Matthew 14; Luke 6; Luke 22; Luke 5).

We had such a moment on that hilltop. When we descended and returned to the car, I found someone had taken and busted out the back window of my car. Dean immediately said, "Don't let this steal your joy." I found the moment paralleled to other times in my life, times when I was on the mountaintop, only to return to reality and have a dream shattered. Satan certainly attacks with this same pattern.

Those mountaintop experiences prepare us to return to the valleys. Regardless of whether we are on the mountain or in the valley, he is always with us.

> My help comes from the Lord, the Maker of
> heaven and earth. (Psalm 121:1–2)

⟡

CHAPTER 17

A Prisoner of Christ

"Welcome to Calvary Chapel. I'm Pastor Dean. Let's just get one thing out of the way if you are new here tonight because it is going to come up. I was able to do thirteen years on a full-ride scholarship in a gated community at Penn State. Oh, I mean the state pen." [The congregation laughed]. Dean smiled sweetly and chuckled. He then continued to speak; it was the Wednesday night service.

"I am so privileged that I am able, somebody like me, to get up here and share the word of God to you, and I must remember that I get to do this. I remember one time when I was at Penn State. I was a Pastor of an inmate church, and it was my turn to bring the message. I did not want to bring the message, and we got locked down. Sergeant walked by, and I asked, 'Are we going to have church tonight? Because I have to bring the message if we do.'

"He answered, 'Dean, you're looking at this all wrong. You don't have to, you get to.'

"This is a privilege. I get to do this! I was only out of prison six months when they handed me the keys to this church. I remember thinking, *What are they thinking?*

"I would go help people haul hay, and people would try to pay me. I would say, "No, no, don't pay me," thinking, *I'm a good guy.* I was thinking, *I don't want your money, but tell all the neighbors what a good guy I am.* I would never admit that I was a sinner. I'm better than that guy. I think God grades on a curve. I'll make it.

"We are going to go down the Romans Road. Church, open your Bibles and let's go to the book of Romans. Romans 3:10: 'There is none righteous, no, not one.' That means me, and that means you. Romans 3:23 says, 'For all have sinned and fall short of the glory of God.' Every one of us, all of us, have sinned. For some reason, I thought I was the exception. Maybe tonight, you think you are the exception. I don't care if you're Billy Graham, the pope, the president of the United States…all have sinned. All of us. None of us are good enough. Romans 6:23: 'The wages of sin is death.' That is what I deserve: death, eternal separation from God. That is what I deserve. God is holy, just, and good, and I am none of the above. Romans 5:8: 'God demonstrates his own love towards us that while we still sinners, Christ died for us.' See, there had to be a payment made. That payment had to be made. Look at it. God demonstrates. Not that he demonstrated, but God demonstrates that love to you and sent his Son to die on a cross at Calvary to pay for mine and your sins, demonstrates his love towards us, that while we were sinners, Christ died for us. Romans 10:9: 'That if you confess with your mouth the Lord Jesus and believe in your heart, you will be saved.' Confess and believe that Jesus died for you. Now that is some good news. I have a good God that loves me.

"I used to say, 'Jesus is Lord.' Lord means one with authority over others. He had no authority in my life. I must confess my allegiance to Christ and Christ alone. You see, it is not about me, and it never has been about me, and it never will be about me. It is all about the Lord Jesus Christ. I had to take Dean off the throne and put the Lord Jesus Christ on the throne.

"I used to train horses. I remember once, I was in the round pen, and I told my son J.R., 'Watch. This horse is going to drop his head, lick his lips, and walk up to me.' I stood in the center of the round pen and would snap the whip and kept that horse running in circles. When I stopped, I turned my back to the horse. The horse dropped his head, licked his lips, and walked up to my back. You see, God had to put me in the round pen. My round pen was prison. I had to run in circles until I was ready to drop my head and bow to God. In Philippians, Paul wrote that he is a bondservant of Jesus

Christ. A bondservant was a slave (a prisoner) to his master. I was a prisoner of the state department of corrections. Now I am a prisoner (a bondservant) of Jesus Christ."

At the end of the service, Dean gave an invitation for those wanting to accept Jesus Christ. I've watched my husband preach time and time again, and I still sit in the pew, amazed at what the Lord has done. I know multiple people that seek out Dean for biblical counsel; they tell me that he "gets them." A wild drinking cowboy, a prisoner, a womanizer turned into a disciple of Christ.

I'm reminded of the other men Jesus chose. Saul (Paul) was a murderer of Christians. Moses was a murderer. David was a murderer and an adulterer. Noah drank too much. Lazarus was dead, and Jesus used him.

Then there were the twelve disciples. Peter denied Christ, three times to be exact. James and John were known for their temper; Christ called them the sons of thunder. Jesus took fishermen and made them "fishers of men" (Mark 1:17). Jesus and these twelve men changed the world.

EPILOGUE

A God of Restoration

Dean is on staff as an assistant pastor with Calvary Chapel in New Mexico. Pastor Ray brought Dean on staff a little over a year after his discharge from prison. Dean leads up several ministries in the church, including the New Thirst Addiction Ministry, jail ministry, and the Calvary Chapel Bible school. He continues to serve in the ministry with Pastor Ray.

Kathleen is on staff with a private school associated with Calvary Chapel. She still works under Pastor Shaun. She is an instructional coach and still teaches occasionally as distinguished emeritus associate professor at the university level.

At the time of this publication, Dean and Kathleen have been married thirty-three years. Dean refuses to subtract the eight years (the divorced years) from the thirty-three. He only acknowledges the original wedding date, December 29, 1990, counting the divorced years as a detour. They both claim that God loved them enough to use prison. They have a strong marriage and counsel other couples struggling in their marriages.

Coy is married. He is employed in Texas as a K-9 officer and SWAT. He and his wife have two boys. Coy reestablished a relationship with his dad. He called one spring and asked his mom and dad to come for spring break. He now calls his dad weekly. They enjoy camping and hunting together.

J.R. is married. He serves full-time in the mission field with his wife. They serve in Muslim territories. They have two boys and one girl. They are courageous and fearless for the gospel. J.R. has been beaten and gassed. They were at a prayer house when the building adjacent was bombed (he, his wife, and children). God continues to protect and use them.

C.J. is married and works for the city of Oklahoma. His wife is a schoolteacher. They have three girls. They attend church in their community. Dean has never met C.J. and his family, although Kathleen claims them as her own. C.J. reestablished a relationship with both of his parents. His mother and stepdad reside in Oklahoma. His mother is a Christian and walking with Christ. She thanked Kathleen for stepping in and helping to raise C.J. She lovingly welcomes Kathleen as part of the family.

Kathleen and her sister Kay have healed their relationship. Kathleen sent a text to her sister one day, apologizing for any hurt she caused. Kay responded. They have been in communication ever since. Kay is active in church in her community and recently invited Kathleen to come to Arizona for a conference.

Kathleen's and Dean's parents are in communication. She visits and calls them. Dean's parents returned all the items they saved, even the truck and trailer. They had kept everything for Dean's return home, boxes and boxes of items. For thirteen years, they stored everything, waiting for his release.

Dean's sister and Kathleen's brother have reunited with the family. They visit a couple of times a year.

The business owner from church that refused to hire or interview Dean came to Dean and apologized. He claimed God had convicted him. He said he had a policy at work to never hire people with a record. He handed Dean a cash gift and told him to take Kathleen out. Dean and Kathleen used the money to attend a Christian marriage conference with all expenses paid.

Follow Kathleen's blog at https://christandprisonerswife.blogspot.com.

⸻ ❦ ⸻

FINAL NOTE

There is a story in the Bible in the book of Joshua. In the story, Joshua stacked twelve stones as a remembrance of God's divine intervention. The Israelites had crossed the Jordan River by God's help to the promised land. The twelve stones served as a lasting memorial of what the Lord had done. This book serves as my stones of remembrance. While many of the memories still bring me sadness, I know the ending and God had the victory.

The story never disclosed Dean's charges, this was intentional. There are several reasons. First, there were other parties involved. The intent was to not cause harm in any way. Second, prison guests are advised not to ask an inmates' charges, and prisoners' wives do not ask each other about their loved one's charges. The charges really do not matter to the story. Finally, this book was written to encourage others as they walk through difficult seasons in their life. If God can save Dean and his family, he can save any family. God can take the mess and turn it into a message for his glory.

After prison, Dean was employed, the organization submitted a background check. Dean was honest about his past and what the background check would state. However, when the report came back, the report stated, "No record found." I was immediately reminded of the scripture in Psalm (103:11–12): "For as the heaven is high above the earth, so great is His mercy toward them that fear Him. As far as the east is from the west, so far hath he removed our transgressions from us." God had forgiven Dean. Whether or not the background check found a record, it did not really matter. In the world, Dean was guilty, but in Christ, he was forgiven. When Dean goes to heaven, his name will be in the Book of Life, and as for the guilty charges, there will be no record found.

APPENDIX

The Fellowship of the Unashamed

I am part of the fellowship of the unashamed. I have Holy Spirit power.

The die has been cast. I have stepped over the line. The decision has been made. I am a disciple of his. I won't look back, let up, slow down, back away, or be still.

My past is redeemed. My present makes sense. My future is secure. I'm finished with low living, sight walking, small planning, smooth knees, colorless dreams, tamed visions, worldly talking, cheap giving, and dwarfed goals.

I no longer need preeminence, prosperity, position, promotions, applause, or popularity. I don't have to be right, first, top, recognized, praised, regarded, or rewarded. I now live by faith, lean on his presence, walk by patience, am uplifted by prayer, and labor by power.

My pace is set. My gait is fast. My goal is heaven. My road is narrow, my way rough, my companions few. My guide is reliable, and my mission is clear.

I cannot be bought, compromised, detoured, lured away, turned back, deluded, or delayed. I will not flinch in the face of sacrifice, hesitate in the presence of the adversary, negotiate at the table of the enemy, pander at the pool of popularity, or meander in the maze of mediocrity.

I won't give up, shut up, let up until I've stayed up, stored up, prayed up, paid up, preached up for the cause of Christ.

I am a disciple of Jesus. I must go till he comes, give 'til I drop, preach till all know, and work till he stops me. And when he comes for his own, he'll have no problem recognizing me. My banner will be clear.

REFERENCES

Women of the Bible

Chapter 2
Leah, Genesis 29–30
Chapter 3
Ruth, the book of Ruth
Chapter 4
Samaritan Woman, the Woman at the Well, John 4
Chapter 6
Widow's Mite, Mark 12
Chapter 7
Hannah, 1 Samuel
Chapter 8
Gomer, Hosea
Chapter 12
Rahab, Joshua 2–3
Chapter 16
Martha, Luke 10

Ephesians 4:31–32

Chapter 6
Mark 12:41–44

Chapter 7
1 Samuel 1–3
2 Corinthians 5:17

Chapter 8
2 Corinthians 5:17
Hosea

Chapter 11
1 Corinthians 7:16
Galatians 6:9

Chapter 12
Jude 1:23

Chapter 13
Ephesians 5:31

Chapter 14
Ecclesiastes 3:1–8
Isaiah 55:8
Ephesians 2:4
Revelation 12:11
Galatians 6:14
Mark 5:9
1 Thessalonians 5:11, 14

Chapter 15
1 Kings 19:8
Genesis 7:4
Genesis 8:3–8

Exodus 24:18
Matthew 4:1–2
Acts 1:3
Luke 15:22–24, 28, 30
2 Corinthians 5:17
Romans 3:9–10, 22, 23

Chapter 16

Luke 10
Nahum 1:7
John 16:33
Psalm 46:1
Psalm 59:16
Psalm 5:15
Psalm 116:16
Psalm 142
Isaiah 61:1
Luke 4:18
Luke 4, 6, 22, 5
Matthew 14
Mark 6
Psalm 121:1–2

Chapter 17

Romans 3:10, 23
Romans 10:9
Romans 5:8

Epilogue

Joshua 4

REFERENCES

Anonymous. Attributed to an African pastor. 1920–1940. *Fellowship of Unashamed.*

Brooks, Garth, and Kent Blazy. 1989. *If Tomorrow Never Comes.* Capitol Nashville.

Casting Crowns. 2005. *I'll Praise You in the Storm.* Beach Street Records.

Cottrell, Travis. 2011. *I Come Broken, Just as I Am.* Worship Together.

English Standard Bible. 2001. Crossway Bibles.

King CJ Bible. 2017. Cambridge University Press.

Lane, Olivia. 2021. *Woman at the Well.* Lane Train Music.

Nelson, Thomas. 2022. *New Spirit-Filled Bible.* New King CJ Version. Thomas Nelson, Inc.

New International Bible. 2011. Zondervan.

Nibauhr, Reinhold. 1930. *Serenity Prayer.*

Our Daily Bread. 2005. Grand Rapids, MI: Our Daily Bread Ministries. August 19, 2005.

Oxford American Dictionary, 3rd ed. 2010. Oxford University Press.

Paulsen, Gary. 2006. *Hatchet.* Simon & Schuster.

Peterson, Eugene. 2002. *The Message Bible.* NavPress.

Piper, John. 2019. *Let Go of the Life You Wanted.* www.desiringgod.org.

Ries, Raul. 2008. *7 Steps to a Successful Marriage.* Somebody Loves You Publishing.

Sanders, Oswald. 2017. *Spiritual Leadership: Principles of Excellent for Every Believer.* Moody Publishers.

Smith, Chuck. 1993. *The Calvary Distinctives.* Word for Today Publishing.

Smith, Chuck. 2001. *Living Water: The Power of the Holy Spirit in Your Life*. Word for Today Publishing.

Smith, Chuck. 2012. *The Philosophy of Ministry of Calvary Chapel*. Word for Today Publishing.

Snicket, Lemony, and Brett Helquist. 1999. *Tale of Unfortunate Events*. Harper Collins.

Stevenson, Mary. 1936. *Footprints in the Sand*.

Weaver, Mike. 2015. *My Story*. Fervent Records.

Webster's New World Dictionary, 5th ed. 2016. William Morrow Paperback.

West, Matthew. 2012. *Forgiveness*. Anthem Entertainment.

White, Sylvie, and Teena Booth. 2010. *Amish Grace*. Lifetime Movie Network.

FOOTPRINTS IN THE SAND

By Mary Stevenson 1936

One night, I dreamed I was walking along the beach with the Lord. Many scenes from my life flashed across the sky. In each scene, I noticed footprints in the sand. Sometimes there were two sets of footprints; other times there was one set of footprints. This bothered me because I noticed that during the low periods of my life, when I was suffering from anguish, sorrow, or defeat, I could see only one set of footprints. So I said to the Lord, "You promised me, Lord, that if I followed you, you would walk with me always. But I have noticed that during the most trying periods of my life, there has only been one set of footprints in the sand. Why, when I needed you most, you have not been there for me?"

The Lord replied, "The times when you have seen only one set of footprints is when I carried you."

ABOUT THE AUTHOR

Kathleen Donalson Tayler is an American speaker and author. Tayler has a blog to encourage women in their daily lives through biblical truths. She has been an educator for more than three decades. She serves at Calvary Chapel with her husband. She is involved in Christian education, addiction recovery, and prison ministries. Kathleen and her husband are the proud parents of two boys and five grandchildren. They live in New Mexico.

www.ingramcontent.com/pod-product-compliance
Lightning Source LLC
Chambersburg PA
CBHW020542160726
47991CB00002B/542